NANNY, MA & ME

Jade Jordan is a mixed-race Irish actor for theatre and film. She is a graduate of Bow Street Academy. She has appeared on Channel 4's *The Virtues* and BBC's *Doctors* and in *You Are Not My Mother*, a feature film by Kate Dolan. Jade has performed in numerous stage plays for the Abbey Theatre, the Druid Theatre Company and Ark Theatre Dublin. Her short film *The Colour Between*, which premiered in summer 2021, was funded by Screen Ireland as part of The Actor as Creator initiative and sees Jade as one of the first Black women to write, produce and star in their own short film.

Dominique Jordan was born in London. She moved to Dublin in her teens where she is still based. She has two daughters.

Kathleen Jordan was born in Dublin in 1932. She moved to London in the late 1950s to become a nurse and returned to Dublin in the 1970s where she is still based. She has three children, eight grandchildren and one great-grandchild all of whom she loves dearly.

Some of the names and details within this book have been changed to respect the privacy of individuals.

NANNY, MA & ME

AN IRISH STORY OF FAMILY, RACE AND HOME

KATHLEEN, DOMINIQUE & JADE JORDAN

HACHETTE
BOOKS
IRELAND

First published in Ireland in 2021 by HACHETTE BOOKS IRELAND

1

Cataloguing in Publication Data is available from the British Library

ISBN 9781529365009

Typeset in ArnoPro by Bookends Publishing Services, Dublin

Printed and bound in Great Britain by Clays, Elcograf S.p.A

Hachette Books Ireland policy is to use papers that are natural, renewable and recyclable products and made from wood grown in sustainable forests. The logging and manufacturing processes are expected to conform to the environmental regulations of the country of origin.

Hachette Books Ireland
8 Castlecourt Centre
Castleknock
Dublin 15, Ireland

A division of Hachette UK Ltd
Carmelite House, 50 Victoria Embankment, EC4Y 0DZ

www.hachettebooksireland.ie

This book is dedicated to the memory of Joseph Jordan,
beloved brother, uncle and great-uncle,
who played a massive part in our lives
and is much missed.

CONTENTS

Prologue

JADE

The uniformed police officer appears to be emotionless, almost bored. I can see his expression, but it tells me nothing. He could be sitting on a park bench, staring into the middle distance. But he's not. He's jamming his knee into the neck of a man pinned to the ground. His colleagues are leaning on the man's torso, grinding his face into the pavement.

I hear the man cry once for his mother and then repeatedly gasp that he can't breathe. I am in my apartment in Castleknock, Dublin in Ireland, watching horror footage from the streets of Minneapolis, Minnesota in the United States at the end of May 2020.

The man on the ground is George Floyd, a forty-six-year-old Black man who went to his local store, Cup Foods, for cigarettes. A teenage shop assistant has called police alleging that Floyd paid for the cigarettes using a fake twenty-dollar bill. Minutes after the first squad car arrives at the scene, George Floyd is face down, handcuffed, pinned beneath white police officers and pleading for his life. Police officer Derek Chauvin takes up position, kneeling on Floyd's neck. Sixteen times, Floyd can be heard gasping that he cannot breathe.

The officers call for medical assistance, yet Chauvin continues to kneel on Floyd's neck. Floyd's eyes close, and it's clear he has fallen unconscious, and still Chauvin doesn't budge.

'Look at him!' a bystander shouts, referring to Floyd's unconscious state. 'Get off him now!'

For the first time, we see a flash of emotion from Chauvin. His face twists in anger, and he pulls a can of Mace from his belt to threaten the restless crowd. The onlookers are growing more distressed and vocal.

'Bro, he's not fucking moving,' a voice in the crowd warns. I can hear a woman's voice say, 'Did they fucking kill him?' Chauvin still kneels on Floyd's neck. 'Check his pulse!' a bystander pleads.

Officer Chauvin is not in fear of his life. He is deliberate and controlled as the minutes tick by. He has one hand stuck casually in his pocket as he jams his knee into Floyd's neck. Chauvin's fellow officers are looking on, unconcerned about the welfare of the unconscious man face down on the street.

An ambulance arrives on the scene. 'Get off his neck!' an onlooker shouts. Chauvin still has his knee on Floyd's neck as the paramedic reaches for the same man's neck to feel for a pulse. Chauvin doesn't remove his knee until the paramedics ask him to do so – a full minute and twenty seconds after they arrive at the scene.

By now, Chauvin has been kneeling on the man's neck

for eight minutes and forty-six seconds. It's his indifference to a man's life, his disdain for a fellow human being, that is so difficult to take. The police officer coldly and calculatedly squeezes the life out of a man over a twenty-dollar bill. What I've been watching, what the world has been watching, is a murder in progress for nearly nine minutes. We are viewing the modern-day equivalent of a lynching. As the video ends and life around me resumes, I am reeling. I feel sick, horrified and furious.

The killing of George Floyd and the protests over his murder take place as I'm learning about and documenting my family history. This process is harder than I thought it would be. I'm talking to Nanny and Ma, asking questions, probing their pasts, and I'm shocked to discover what they went through. I'm a Black Irish woman, the daughter of another Black Irish woman who struggled for a long time because of her skin colour. I'm the granddaughter of another woman exposed to the icy winds of society because she loved and married a Black man and had three Black children.

I don't know what I expected to find out, but I often feel angry while writing this book. These women are people I love, and nobody should have to go through what they went through. I'm upset that people mistreated my family for no other reason than their skin colour. I wonder how people can be so cruel.

The rollercoaster of feelings I've been experiencing

become more intense as the harrowing scenes of George Floyd's death are revealed to me on my laptop screen. I'm still bewildered by how badly my nanny was treated. I'm sad about what Ma has gone through in her life. Now, I'm appalled watching the pitiless face of that police officer in Minneapolis. This indifference to suffering floors me. I despair at the levels of hatred that drive one man to suffocate another or one family to make outcasts of their own.

Haunted by this rolling news, consumed by the casual cruelty, I start scrolling through comments on social media about the killing of George Floyd and the ensuing riots in Minneapolis. How are other people making sense of this? I see that some people of colour and people from different ethnicities in Ireland feel prompted to share their own experiences. They reveal the indignities they've encountered because of the colour of their skin. Though the incidents they talk about are not life-threatening, they are still degrading and hateful. They shouldn't happen to anyone. Yet I see their experiences brushed aside by other commenters, some of whom even dismiss suggestions that racism exists in Ireland.

The violent end to George Floyd's life sparks a conversation about racism around the world, and still that reaction persists here, in Ireland: that racism is not something that affects people in the country where I live. *We're grand – nothing to see here.* I feel raw, like an exposed nerve. I can't believe the number of people who don't believe discrimination happens here. And in the days and weeks that follow, I sit and think about it. Well, maybe that's because they aren't Black or brown and have never experienced racism. And that gets me thinking. If people haven't seen discrimination or understood what they're seeing, how would they know that it's a problem? How can we address or even discuss the problem?

Comments like 'Cop on! Ireland is nothing like America' stick in my head.

True, we don't commonly see the graphically violent racism that exists in America. But we don't have to view racism through the prism of the American experience. Just because we don't see the kind of systematic police savagery exhibited in the death of George Floyd doesn't mean there aren't other forms of discrimination in Ireland.

Racism is an issue that I didn't want to speak about for a long time. It's much nicer to believe that we live in a fair and equal world than in a world with discrimination and prejudice. I know people don't want to hear the truth. We like to boast 'sure, Ireland's a multicultural society now', as if we're all holding hands around the campfire and playing happy families.

But people of colour in this country know it's not like that at all. I know all about racism because, like many others, I've experienced it. Emotional and physical wounds are being inflicted on people of colour every day in this country. Some like me are born Irish, others are new Irish citizens, some are in Ireland on work or student visas, and others are asylum seekers. They are all people, all worthy of being treated with respect and dignity. Many times, they are not. And I know all about having your self-esteem unpicked, piece by piece, slur by slur.

At this juncture, I need to state that I'm the only one in my immediate family who feels the need to talk about this or talk about our history. I'm the awkward person in the room confronting things, poking around, asking questions. It has been a struggle at times to get my nanny and ma to open up, but when they have, their recollections have blown my mind. My family story certainly shines a spotlight on a darker side of Irish society. It contains some bitter truths that should end any misconceptions that racism does not exist in Ireland.

Maybe it's a generational thing, but my nanny shrugs off her experiences and excuses cruelties by saying they were the times she lived in. Most of the time, when I ask her about something, she says she doesn't remember. I sometimes suspect that 'not remembering' is convenient. It means she'd rather forget.

My ma is equally stoic and insists the negative experiences she faced were like 'water off a duck's back'. But she can't stop the tell-tale tears that run down her face as she recalls some episodes in her past. I know what happened affected their entire lives. Race has shaped my ma's life and my nanny's life, and it shouldn't have.

But they would both prefer to forget what they experienced, to sweep it under the carpet. My ma has even said that the past belongs in the past. But I think I have a right to know what went on because it's my history too, and it's part of who I am. I also think there's a real value in confronting the ghosts of the past. Tackling these issues, even if it means opening old wounds, is an opportunity for us to heal.

As an actor, I had often thought about writing my family story, and I've always had a dream to make that story into a film. So, back in 2016, I started the project by interviewing my nanny on video. Then life took over, and I got busy, and my family story got pushed aside. Writing this book only became a project in earnest during the Covid-19 lockdown in 2020 when I was left with more time to work on it. And even then, it was only after the death of George Floyd in May of that year that I felt really compelled to tell our story.

As I started delving into my family history, I also started thinking about my future and Ireland's future. If I ever have kids, I don't want them to experience what their great-grandmother, their grandmother and their mother went through. History is history, and we can't change it, but we can make things better. I don't want any child to feel demeaned or alienated because of the colour of their skin. I want children to grow up in blissful ignorance of a time when police officers murdered innocent people like George Floyd because of the colour of their skin. I never want them to experience fear, prejudice or being called 'n***ers' or 'Pakis' by strangers on the street.

If we're honest, we can all admit there is some racism, sexism and bigotry deep within us. But I know I can learn to be a better person. We all can learn if we're willing to open our minds and open our mouths and speak out when we see injustice. Any country can become bigoted and intolerant if good people choose to do nothing. I want children to grow up in a kind, inclusive and broad-minded society. And I want them to have lives where they have equal opportunities along with friends and colleagues of all colours. I believe we can bring about a cultural transformation regarding racism if we speak out about it; if we highlight the way things are, the behaviours of certain people, and challenge them. Discrimination and conscious and unconscious bias in Ireland are things that we need to talk about – often and loudly, in a conversation that involves everyone.

Because when we remain silent in the face of racist behaviour, we're no different to those police officers in Minneapolis. We are indifferent to other people's suffering; we turn a blind eye to the 'knee on the neck' of the marginalised around us. Every one of us can be an activist. We can stand up for racial equality and call out injustice when we see it. We can all play a crucial role in creating an equal society.

Resistance starts at home, so this story is my contribution. I am telling one family's story – my family's story – hoping it fosters awareness of the vibrant Black and Irish community in my country. This story is the result of long hours of delving into the colourful pasts of my nanny and my ma. I hope by relating what I learned from their narratives, it will give some insight into the experiences, the struggles and the everyday life of one family of colour in Ireland today. Most of all, I just want to start a conversation, because once people come together to talk, the possibilities are endless.

Kathleen

SAINT PATRICK'S

When I was twenty-one, they put me into Saint Patrick's, a 'mental asylum' as they were called in those days, but I prefer to call it a psychiatric hospital. Trying to recall details from that time is like struggling to think of a word: images flitting around in my head, words wavering on the tip of my tongue, I can't quite see the whole picture. It frustrates me, but I don't remember a lot from back then. *There's no point in asking me questions like that, Jade, because I remember so little about being there.*

Time slipped by. I don't remember how long I was in there, but I do remember this. I came around one day to find my mother standing by my bed with Dr Lynch. Tom Lynch was in his early thirties and such a handsome man with dark hair flopping over his forehead. He had an intense gaze as if he was looking into your soul. It's funny how I can see him so clearly even though I remember so little about everything else. When my mother and Dr Lynch realised that I was awake and watching them, they turned to me.

'Now, Kathleen,' Dr Lynch said in that slow and calm voice

he reserved for patients, 'I was just saying to your mother that you've been here a long time, and I think it's time we transfer you to Stewarts Hospital.'

His soothing words rolled around my brain, along with the dull ache and the fog. *Stewarts Hospital? Why did they want me to go there?* I felt a little confused. I'd never heard of the hospital before. Dr Lynch must have seen some alarm in my face.

'It's a nice place, Kathleen, lovely and quiet,' he assured me. 'It would be good for you to rest there for a while until you're feeling fully better.'

Half of me, the exhausted side and the part of me that liked to please people, especially my mother, wanted to nod and agree. But somewhere deep within me, something told me to resist. They call it intuition, don't they? I must have somehow known that this was an important crossroads. If I was to leave Saint Patrick's, I knew what I needed to do, so I turned to my mother.

'I want to go home,' I said.

Those few words may have been the most significant I've ever spoken because if I had agreed to go to Stewarts Hospital back then, I might still be there today. Years later, I found out more about Stewarts Hospital and discovered it was a long-term residential institution for those with intellectual disabilities.

My time behind the high walls of the Saint Patrick's Mental

Hospital in Dublin remains a blur. I don't have any memories of passing through those big iron gates on Bow Lane all those years ago. I've seen them since, and I wonder how I could have forgotten that forbidding entrance. When I was admitted to the hospital in 1953, the place had barely changed in its two-hundred-year history. It was built as Saint Patrick's House for *Imbeciles*. Wasn't that an awful term to describe a human being? Its founder, Jonathan Swift, was just as insensitive when he described it as a home 'for fools and the mad'.

I've heard people say Saint Patrick's was gloomy and damp, and others speak about the echoing corridors and the iron bars on every window. My hazy memory of the place is not like that at all. It was a private hospital then, and I had my own room, and even though there was nothing much in it, it was a pleasant room. Dr Lynch and the staff were kind. I didn't have a sense of being locked up. It always seemed like I had the freedom to come and go as I liked. In my mind, it remains a nice place, even though I know some things that happened to me were not very nice.

I'm told they gave me electroconvulsive therapy (ECT) or 'shock therapy', that they placed electrodes on either side of my forehead and sent an electric charge through my brain. Back then, they did it without anaesthetic. I believe they often needed up to six strong nurses to hold the patients down, and the current was so strong that patients were shocked into unconsciousness or convulsions. The muscle contractions could be so violent that patients were often injured from crush fractures in their backs. God, can you imagine? I suppose they could be awfully cruel in those days. I have no recollection of anyone sending electric charges through my brain, but they say I lost my memory during the treatment, so that may explain it.

A defence mechanism? I suppose memory loss could be a defence mechanism, something to help forget the terrible trauma of it all. Maybe that's true, Jade, but I'll never know that for sure, will I?

They prescribed shock treatment in cases of deep depression then. They used it to relieve tension and 'shock' patients out of their dream worlds and catatonic states. I don't know if it worked. They rarely do this kind of thing to psychiatric patients now, and if it's done, they use anaesthetic, which has to be a good thing.

They don't do lobotomies any more either, but I still have two holes in the top of my head from where they did it to me. Nearly seventy years later, I can still feel the two deep indents in my skull from where they drilled into my brain. They told me it was an operation called a 'leucotomy', and they explained that the doctors cut the nerve fibres in my brain to relieve the tension they felt I was experiencing. That's how they used to explain it in those days anyway. Whenever medical people asked about the holes in my head over the years, I always explained that I'd had a leucotomy. But a few years ago, I was in James Connolly Memorial Hospital. *I don't know why they dropped the 'James' and 'Memorial' from the name. They call it Connolly Hospital now, don't they, Jade?* After a fall, I ended up in the hospital, and the consultant corrected me when I called it a leucotomy. She was on her rounds, and in front of everyone, she said it was a pre-frontal lobotomy. I thought it was a bit rude of her to contradict me in front of all those people, but that's what she did. *She must have been showing off because you looked it up, didn't you, Jade? And don't they mean the very same thing anyway?*

I don't remember any of it, but the staff in Saint Patrick's must have brought me to the Richmond Hospital for the lobotomy because that's where they did those operations. A doctor called Mr Adams Andrew McConnell was known to specialise in the procedure there. God help us, but those operations were sometimes fatal. In the public mental hospital, Grangegorman, sixty or seventy poor souls were given lobotomies, and several died as a result. Others were so severely injured that they could never be released from the hospital.

They used to say that the operation restored calmness and helped make the patients placid. I think they treated us like guinea pigs. They used to try all these things without any scientific proof that they helped anyone. Educated people like doctors had too much power then because no one questioned them. I was lucky I wasn't left permanently disabled.

I should never have had that operation or that electric shock treatment. I was an adult, and I'm sure I didn't give permission. I often wonder who gave permission for them to do those things, or if they just went ahead and did them anyway? I'm just glad that they don't allow them to do those procedures any more.

I remember the day I left Saint Patrick's, at least. My mother arrived wearing a navy suit with a pencil skirt and gloves. She always looked so smart and elegant. I made an effort to look cheerful because I never meant to be a bother to my lovely mother. But did you ever get a blow to the head? That's the feeling I had. I was dazed and confused, and I wondered where my father was. I worshipped my father, and even though he had ten other children, he adored me too. We were the closest and the best of friends. As a child, wherever my father went, you would find me right behind him.

'Where's Daddy?' I asked my mother that day. 'Is he not coming?'

I expected him to follow her into the hospital room any minute. Instead, my mother flinched, like I'd smacked her, a shadow crossing her face.

'Your father is dead, Kathleen. You know he's gone, love. We need to stop doing this.'

Her words came like a punch to my gut. Yet, somewhere deep inside me, I knew she was speaking the truth. I just wanted to forget, and sometimes I was able to forget my father had died. I had forgotten so many things. Why wasn't I allowed to forget this? Tears poured down my face, and my mother pulled me into her arms.

'Oh Lord God, I come to you for help and succour,' my mother prayed. 'Give me grace to bear my child's affliction with patience and strength. Bless me, oh Father, and restore my child Kathleen Patricia Mary Jordan to health. In the name of Your Holy Son, Jesus Christ. Amen.'

She muttered this prayer again and again into my hair, her breath hot on my head. Finally, she lifted her head and fiercely gripped my face in her hands.

'With the help of God, you will get through this, child. But you have to promise me that you won't ask where your father is any more.'

'I promise, Mother,' I said, and I wiped away my tears with the backs of my hands. 'I won't forget again.' And I didn't.

One of my last memories of Saint Patrick's is a girl called Mary. How is it that I still recall her name when I can't remember much else? She was only my age, maybe twenty-one or twenty-two, and she shuffled up and down the corridor outside my room all day. She would have done it all night too if she was let. She had long, dark, straight hair, big dark eyes and a white moon face. She was such a pretty girl. All day, she made her way up and down, up and down that draughty corridor. She was a solicitor's daughter, they said.

'Goodbye, Mary,' I said as I was going, but her expression was blank and her eyes vacant. I don't think she ever saw or heard me. I still see her in my mind's eye, you know. I sometimes wonder what happened to that poor girl and if they ever let her out of that place.

DADDY

Honest to God, it's hard for me to believe that I was a patient in Saint Patrick's for three years. It felt as if I'd been in there for merely a fortnight, yet three years had disappeared from my life. Some memories came back to me from before that time. Or maybe they're memories I've constructed after people told me what had happened. I'm not sure any more.

I remember some things clearly from before my hospital days. My troubles began on a warm summer evening, Wednesday, 6 May 1953. My mother was in the kitchen making the tea, and I was minding my brother Joseph, who had Down syndrome, and a few of the younger ones. Our family home was on Dublin's northside. It was a house with four bedrooms, a kitchen, a pantry and a living room that always flickered with a welcoming fire in winter.

Two Gardaí arrived at our house. I just remember them standing there and knowing that guards at the door were rarely a good sign. Few people had telephones in those days, so the local police station was often called upon to deliver news about accidents, serious illnesses or deaths in a family.

'I'm sorry, Mrs Jordan, but we have a message from the Richmond Hospital asking you to come quickly,' one of the guards said. 'They say your husband has taken a bad turn.'

My father, Joseph, had been suffering for some time from stomach cancer. Still, the guards' message came as a terrible shock for all of us. He'd been operated upon a day earlier, but Mother had been to the hospital to see him that morning, and he had been recovering well. Until that week, Daddy had been going to work every day, and generally, he seemed to be well and coping with the illness.

His cancer was probably the result of a chain-smoking habit of sixty cigarettes a day. Daddy's brand was Craven A, which came in a red and white box with a little black-cat logo on the front. Every birthday and every Christmas, everyone wrapped up packs of cigarettes as a gift for Daddy. That's all he ever got as a present, and I always say that we all helped kill him.

My father was a civil servant, a production manager for Gaeltarra Éireann in Oriel House, Westland Row in Dublin city centre. Gaeltarra Éireann was a state agency that aimed to attract industrial investment into the Irish-speaking Gaeltacht areas. Daddy had to travel a lot for work, as the Gaeltacht areas were in Meath, Galway, Kerry and Donegal. I guess he must have always gone by train because we never had a car, and he never drove.

My father was born on 29 July 1901 over the family shop

on Main Street, Strabane, County Tyrone. Daddy's parents were Patrick and Treasa Jordan, and his father was a cabinet-maker and upholsterer by trade. Patrick and Treasa had two furniture stores, one on Main Street in Strabane and the other on Church Street in Dungannon. By all accounts, the family was well off, and my grandfather was a respected businessman and a trustee of the local bank, the Strabane Loan Fund Society.

But their family fortunes changed when my grandfather died in Dublin in April 1904, before my father reached his third birthday. At least one newspaper printed an obituary, which described the man as 'a well-known Nationalist and Catholic' who 'closely identified with the public life of the town [Strabane].' It also said that he 'had been in declining health and his end was not altogether unexpected'. My grandfather's funeral mass was held in the Capuchin Friars' church, Saint Mary of Angels, on Church Street in Dublin. It seems the family may have settled in Dublin during his long illness. I wonder if they thought they might find better treatment for him there.

It was always said in the family that their furniture stores were burnt out by the British, but I don't know when or *if* that even happened. I remember my father used to say that wherever the British went, they stole, so he was reared with the same nationalist beliefs as his late father.

Joseph Jordan was twenty-four when he married Mary Jane

Drew on 31 August 1925, in Saint Laurence O'Toole Church in Seville Place in Dublin's inner city. His address appears on their marriage cert as 13 Eccles Street, Dublin, and his occupation was listed as a 'post office clerk'.

My mother, Mary, was raised at 23 Ossory Road on Dublin's North Strand and was the daughter of a labourer, Richard Drew, and his wife, Jane. In those years, the city was full of squalor and tenement housing, and many working-class people had to live in overcrowded and unsanitary conditions. Around the time my parents married, the suburb of Marino was being built as Dublin Corporation's first ever major public-housing development. This new 'garden suburb' offered good quality, affordable family homes with lots of parks and gardens. Nearly every house came with amenities like a living room, scullery, larder, bathroom, coal cellar and back and front garden.

My mother and father bought a four-bedroom property in Marino and went on to have twelve children there, eleven of whom survived. From what I know, they had a very happy marriage. I certainly never remember a cross word between them growing up. Their marriage has been a source of amazement to one of my grandsons, Joshua.

'If I ask you something, Nanny, will you tell me the truth?' he asked one day in recent years.

'Of course I will,' I said.

'What was your mother's name?'

'Mary,' I replied.

'What was your father's name?'

'Joseph.'

'Mary and Joseph?' he asked, wide-eyed.

'That's right.'

Joshua blessed himself. 'Daddy told me, but I didn't believe him!' he said.

I was born in 1932, the fourth oldest in the family after three sisters, and they named me after my father's sister, Kathleen. She became a nun and was sent to the foreign missions. Poor Kathleen contracted malaria in some far-off land, and Lord rest her poor soul, she died young, so we never knew her. Next to me was another sister, whose twin brother died at birth, Lord rest his little soul too. Then there was another set of twins, and this time the boy, Joseph, was born with Down syndrome. Then I had three more brothers and a sister.

We had a happy family life and a lovely childhood. We were all sent to private school because there was no free second-level education in those days. I went to the Dominican Convent in Eccles Street, which is gone now and has been taken over by the Mater Hospital.

I finished school when I was eighteen with no thoughts of what I was going to do afterwards. Girls didn't think about work or careers unless they had to back then. *They really didn't, Jade.* My older sisters just got married after school, but I never went to dances, so I never had boyfriends. I was a quiet sort

27

and was content to stay at home, where I had many younger brothers and sisters to help look after. Without all the modern conveniences of washing machines and central heating, there was a lot of work to be done to keep a large family in those days. My mother had the help of a lovely woman, a housemaid called May Dunne, for over a decade.

Shopping was a different experience then. No one had refrigerators or freezers so the local butcher's, Broughs, used to send a boy from Glandore Road off Griffith Avenue to take our meat order every day. We went down to the shop every Friday to settle the bill.

There were no sliced pans in the shops either, but my mother baked her bread then. Tea-bags or even packets of tea-leaves didn't exist. When I went to our local grocer's store and dairy shop, Mr Connolly weighed out a quarter pound of loose tea on the scales and scooped it into a brown paper bag. He sliced our butter from a large golden block stored on ice and wrapped it in greaseproof paper.

Youngsters today think it's unbelievable, but growing up, there was no such thing as toilet rolls either. We cut up newspapers and plain brown wrapping paper, put a string through the paper slips and hung them on a hook beside the toilet. It was a form of recycling long before it was fashionable.

We used to call to Mrs Ryan's newsagent's for packs of

Craven A for Daddy, but she also sold loose cigarettes to her customers. 'Me ma sent me down for a cigarette, Mrs Ryan,' young lads used to lie so they could share a smoke down the laneways after school.

Even though there were eleven of us children, I still remember how we were spoiled every Christmas. Daddy had a tradition of leading us down the stairs every Christmas morning for our presents. The Christmas pudding was laid on the sideboard, and a piece of it was always missing.

'Santy can never resist your mother's pudding,' my father always said.

I'm sure money must have been tight, but they always managed to buy a wonderful present for each of us. One year, for example, all the girls got Crolly dollies, and one was nicer than the next. There was a huge demand for these handmade dolls from Donegal. Queues used to form outside the stores at Christmas whenever they expected a delivery. I don't know how they managed to get dolls for all us girls, but they did. Maybe Daddy managed to get them from the factory through his connections with the Donegal Gaeltacht.

I had lovely dresses then too. I remember a yellow winter dress with a small print that everyone admired when I wore it. I also had a gorgeous red tartan dress with a white collar that I loved. People looked after their clothes, passed them down through the family and kept them for years then. Mother wore a long apron to protect her clothes all day, and before my father came home after five o'clock, she would change into a half apron that went around her trim waist.

My father was a small man who was always immaculately dressed in a suit and a waistcoat. He wouldn't step outside the door without his trilby hat and his coat. He was such a kind man. I can never remember him raising his voice in the house, even with so many children.

But our lovely life was shattered that May evening when those Gardaí arrived. I remember it so clearly. It was ten to six on a Wednesday, and my stomach felt sick as my mother and I grabbed our coats and handbags. Mother brought my little brother Jim with us, Lord rest his soul. She must have felt that our housekeeper, May, had too many to mind. The guards brought us to the hospital.

The last thing we'd expected was my father becoming seriously ill. Two nights earlier, he and my mother had been to the Savoy Cinema on O'Connell Street to see the Charlie Chaplin movie *Limelight*. I wonder how much of it my father absorbed, considering he was due to have his operation the next day. God love them, they were both probably trying to take their minds off his surgery.

My mother saw Father again two days after his operation and believed he was so well that she said a few of us children could see him the next day. Now, hours after that reassuring visit, she was rushing back to the hospital, with Jim and me in tow, not knowing what to expect.

When we got to the Richmond, we had to wait in the outpatients' department while they checked to see where my father was. I'm not sure what happened next. My mother said I walked away from her while waiting for the nurse to tell us where to go. I don't know how I knew where to go, but I must have felt drawn to my father. I went straight down a hospital corridor and looked into a ward, and I saw him there. I remember that bit clearly. A pile of pillows propped him up, his eyes were shut, and he looked smaller than I'd ever seen him.

Around his bed, I could see one of my sisters. Maybe the guards had called over to her house too. My sister had her head bowed as two nuns fingered their rosary beads and recited the rosary. I knew straight away that my father was dead. They tell me that I let out a blood-curdling scream that was heard all around the hospital, and I collapsed where I stood. I don't remember any of that. All I remember is waking up in my mother's bed the following day.

My father was only fifty-two when he died. His death certificate says he expired from 'postoperative heart failure'. I remember my mother opening a letter that arrived on the Friday morning, the morning of Daddy's funeral. I can see her expression now like a recording in my head. She closed her eyes, and her face crumpled, and she burst into tears before us. We picked up the letter, and it was an itemised bill for Daddy's care from Saint Laurence's Hospital, which the Richmond, Whitworth and Hardwicke hospitals were collectively known as. They couldn't even wait until after his funeral to send us the bill.

That day, Mother left the younger children at home, as adults never brought children to funerals back then. My older siblings and I supported her at Daddy's funeral service in Saint Vincent de Paul Church on Griffith Avenue in Marino. Afterwards, we went to Glasnevin Cemetery, where, to this day, I can still see the gravediggers lowering his oak coffin into the ground.

After that, all my memories seem to disappear. They told me they brought me to see a psychiatrist for a while before I ended up in Saint Patrick's Hospital. I don't know if I was catatonic or hysterical because no one ever explained what symptoms of illness I showed. It must have been the shock. I probably never expected my father to die and was in terrible grief. I was heartbroken, but was a psychiatric hospital the right place for me? I'm not sure.

I don't think I had many visitors in Saint Patrick's. I don't recall my mother ever visiting me, but she was probably busy caring for all the younger children. Joseph needed a lot of minding. He was a runner. If he got out the front door, he bolted, and he was hard to catch. The neighbours and everyone used to run down the road after him in case he got killed on the road.

I remember Mr Miller, a bus driver on the number 30 bus, Lord have mercy on him, found him one time. He was driving the bus through Clontarf, miles down the road from us, and who did he see only Joseph. We were all out looking for him, but Lord bless us, Joseph had already crossed two main roads at that stage. Mr Miller pulled over the bus, and he persuaded Joseph to come on board. There was a conductor on the bus in those days, and Mr Miller warned him to stand over Joseph and not to move from him, even for a fare.

On his way back into town, Mr Miller stopped in Fairview and waited until a number 24 bus came along. He placed Joseph on the number 24 and asked the driver and the conductor to drop him off at our family home. *We were so lucky that Mr Miller was driving the bus that day, weren't we?*

I remember one of my little brothers coming up to see me in Saint Patrick's once. The day stands out in my memory because he arrived sporting a broken leg with a big plaster cast around it, and with a terrible story.

'Kath, I fell off the wall and broke my leg, and they operated on me in Temple Street,' he said, his eyes wide. 'Uncle Jim says they must've been a right shower of eejits who done my leg because when I went back to have the plaster taken off, they said they'd set the leg wrong.'

'No!'

'Yes, and guess what they did?'

'What?'

'They brought me back into Temple Street and broke my leg again!'

'Oh, no!'

'They did, Kath. I swear!'

I'll never forget that story. But vivid memories like this one are rare.

The rest of my time in Saint Patrick's is ... nothing. Just nothing. I must have been lost in a bubble of grief because I still don't know where those three years disappeared to. I was twenty-one when I went in, and I was twenty-four when I came out again. I suppose I had a complete breakdown. I must have had, but like I said, no one ever really talked about it, even when I came home.

I know that there were many more like me because there were thousands in hospitals like that back then. During the 1950s, there were 20,000 residents in psychiatric hospitals in Ireland every night. Ireland had more people in psychiatric hospitals in the world per head of population, even more than the USSR, as Russia was then known.

I don't remember any stigma about being in Saint

Patrick's. *I don't, Jade. There might have been if I was in Grangegorman or Portrane, but I was in a nice private hospital.* My sister Margaret told me about a neighbour who thought my mother was spoiling me.

'You're too soft on her, Mrs Jordan,' she said. 'If you ask me, you should put her in Grangegorman or Portrane. She wouldn't be long about getting well then.'

But my kind mother insisted she didn't resent paying for a private hospital.

'It's her father's money I'm spending, and it's what he would have wanted,' she said.

I suppose that's why I stayed in Saint Patrick's for all those years. But I was very glad to leave. The day I came home, my heart lifted when I saw the familiar terraces as we drove through Fairview and Marino. I remember being so happy and relieved when the hackney pulled up outside our house. I must have doubted that I would get home at all.

My younger brothers and sisters were all excited, leading me to the kitchen where there was an iced cake on the table to welcome me home. But my abiding memory of returning to our house was the smell of smoke. The smell of my father's Craven A cigarettes filled my nostrils as soon as I walked in the door.

At first, I thought maybe someone in the house had taken up smoking since I left, but I soon realised that wasn't the case. My father was three years dead, and the smell of smoke should have been gone, but I could smell his cigarettes as if he were smoking in the room beside us. I asked if anyone else could smell cigarette smoke, and they looked at me strangely.

'You must be smelling the fire in the range,' my mother said. I agreed, and I never brought it up again. But the smell of my father's Craven A cigarettes haunted me through every room in the house.

ENGLAND

I can't explain what it was, but one day I woke up feeling that it was time to go. I felt it was time to leave home. That's the only way to explain it. For two years after Saint Patrick's, I stayed at home, and I quickly fell back into the house routine. Looking after the younger children and doing domestic chores absorbed all my time.

But things weren't the same at home with Daddy gone. Everyone else had three years to adjust, but to me, it was a fresh agony every day to realise I'd never see him again. It felt like the heart of the house was missing. And then there was the constant reminder as that smell of cigarette smoke continued to follow me. No one else smelt it, so that troubled me. I knew it had to be in my head, and my mind was playing tricks on me, but that didn't stop that smell of Craven As.

My older siblings were moving on, marrying and having children, and my younger ones were growing up fast. My mother promised me I didn't need to worry about my future because my father had left the house to me. It seemed ordained that I would stay at home with my mother and brother, Joseph. I loved being home with my family. I would have been content to stay if I didn't have that constant smell of cigarette smoke in my head. It made me feel uneasy all the time.

An advert caught my eye when I was reading the *Evening Herald* one night. I don't remember actively looking for a job, but as soon as I saw the notice in the 'positions offered' column, I read and reread it with growing interest:

Young ladies interested in nursing (over 18 years) required to train as nurses for mental defectives, in a modern, progressive hospital with all amenities. Complete nursing training given. Salary commences at £270 per annum. £40 and £50 bonuses for passing exams. Resident or non-resident as desired. Residential charges £113 pa. Full particulars from Matron, Cell Barnes Hospital, St Albans.

There were always adverts for trainee nurses in England then. There was no reason for this particular advertisement to interest me, except I woke up that morning with this feeling that I had to leave home.

I didn't know anything about Cell Barnes Hospital or the town of Saint Albans in England, but the job stood out from the other nursing jobs because it offered accommodation. *Resident or non-resident as desired.* It gave me the security I needed. I could leave my home in Dublin knowing that I had a roof over my head when I reached England.

Girls were expected to pay hospitals for nursing training in Ireland then. It was a lot of money, and many Irish girls went to the UK as they couldn't afford the schooling here. They could train for free in England as long as they worked in the hospital for at least one year afterwards. The thought of joining the caring profession began to appeal to me. I already cared for Joseph and my other younger siblings, and I wondered why I had never thought of nursing before. I suppose this advert caught my attention because I was ready to go.

I made up my mind almost overnight and wrote an application letter to the matron of Cell Barnes Hospital. Of course, I didn't mention that I had been a so-called 'mental defective' only a few years earlier. My mother was taken by surprise and was hesitant at first.

'Have you thought what might happen if you become … unwell?' she said. 'You know that you'll have no family for support in England.'

But I had so little recollection of those years in Saint Patrick's, and I had been perfectly well since leaving the hospital. My illness seemed so far removed from me that it was like it had happened to another person.

Everything seemed to move very quickly after that. It's odd, but I don't remember my mother the day I was leaving. Daddy's brother, Jim, Lord have mercy on him, brought me to Westland Row Station. *They call it Pearse Street Station now, don't they?* The plan was to travel to Dun Laoghaire, where I would catch the boat to Holyhead.

Of course, there were flights to London in those days, but they weren't for ordinary people. The price of a flight to London in the mid-to-late 1950s was £20 or £30, an entire month's salary or more. You had to be wealthy to go by airplane, so nearly everyone travelled to England by boat. I had my father's old brown suitcase, well-worn and scuffed from all the years he'd been travelling around the country, and I filled it with the few things I had. I stuffed cheese sandwiches in my handbag for the journey too. Uncle Jim made sure to sprinkle holy water over me as I boarded the train.

'Don't forget to write to your mother every week, and let us know how you are getting on, won't you?' he said. I remember looking back at him as the train was pulling out, and he was blessing himself. England was considered a godless and pagan country then, so a single girl travelling there was cause for concern.

I don't remember being in any way nervous about setting out on my own. When you think of it, I should have been. I'd led a very sheltered life until then, and I knew very little about life outside my small part of Dublin. We had no television in those days, so I had no idea what to expect. It was a real step into the unknown to travel anywhere then, but I had just decided this was what I was going to do, and I did it.

When the train pulled into Dun Laoghaire pier, I followed

the hordes of other people carrying cases and bags. Like me, everyone was trying to board the ferry to Holyhead in Wales. I had a steamer reservation ticket clutched tightly in my fist, but there was a sense of urgency about getting on board because there was little control of ticket sales. Hundreds of people were often left stranded on the quays in Dun Laoghaire or Holyhead, waiting for the next day's boat.

The ferry to Holyhead also doubled as the cattle boat and mail boat in those days. Most of the passengers assembled on the deck while the livestock was locked below. It was a breezy April day, and the gulls wheeled and swooped in the bright skies overhead. A kindly middle-aged lady with a headscarf tied tightly under her chin patted a space beside her and offered me a seat on a bench. Most others had to be content to stand around or hang over the side of the ship, watching everyone else make their way up the gangplank. Many started to settle down on bales of goods or took position on the ground with their trunks, suitcases or carpet bags. Some simply carried their belongings in flour sacks. The deck was packed with people of every age, but mostly young men and women hoping for work in England. The tangy salt air mixed with the smell from the cattle who bellowed and bawled in the bowels of the ship.

A ripple of excitement made its way through the passengers as the boat engines began churning and black clouds of smoke started belching through the funnel. The nice lady beside me chatted non-stop while she took a blanket from her basket and flung it over her knees. She had a lemonade bottle full of milk and a mountain of sandwiches wrapped in brown paper.

'Where are you heading, love? Saint Albans? Never heard of it. Is it your first time? Take my advice: stay with your own people, and you'll come to no harm. I know good clean lodgings with a nice Catholic landlady, not far from Euston ...'

Almost as soon as we got out to sea, the sun disappeared, and dark clouds gathered in the open sky overhead. It's hard to believe now, but neither day nor night sailings offered shelter from the wind or rain. The waves began to swell, and as they did, the boat began pitching and heaving. Amid the sounds of the cattle lowing, the passengers' groans rose.

Oh God, in no time at all, everything turned awful. The heavy rolls of the boat and the terrible smell of slurry from below decks proved too much for many. The poor lady beside me fled to the side of the ship to heave her ham sandwiches into the Irish sea. I clutched the bench underneath me so as not to be thrown from it. The spray came in over the sides many times, and there was a chorus of wails each time the saltwater drenched us.

The woman staggered back to her seat beside me, eventually. 'Jesus, Mary and Joseph, save us, protect us,' she recited over and over again. She had rosary beads in one hand, which she kissed every time she made the plea. Others around us muttered earnest prayers too, but some people looked too ill to care whether they lived or died.

Travelling to and from England by boat was a terrible ordeal for Irish people in the fifties and early sixties. The boat service across the Irish Sea was run by British Railways. Even though the Irish government and the Irish Tourist Association constantly complained, the company did nothing to improve conditions. They held a monopoly on the route to England, and without competition, they didn't care. No Irish company could set up a competing travel route because much of the traffic was one way, and British Rail controlled all the trains on the other side of the Irish sea.

The crossing was so rough that the boat docked late, and there was a terrible scramble down the gangplanks onto the station platform at Holyhead. Everyone was determined to pile into the waiting train for Euston Station in London. The carriages were heaving with people, and many stood or sat on their cases the entire journey. It was about six or seven hours to London by steam engine in those days.

My first impression of London was the maze of train tracks, hundreds of tracks, crisscrossing each other as we pulled into Euston Station. I realised this city must be huge compared to my hometown.

The passengers moved almost as one as we poured out onto the bleak railway platform. Most of the Irish voyagers headed for the Kilburn area of the city, known as County Kilburn in those days. It was always said most Irish emigrants chose Kilburn and neighbouring Cricklewood as their base in England because it was as far as anyone wanted to walk from Euston with a suitcase.

I went in a different direction, making my way to Saint Pancras Station, about a quarter of an hour's walk away. I can still recall stopping to stare at the first iconic red double-decker bus I saw along the route. The train from Saint Pancras brought me to Saint Albans, twenty miles outside London. It was early evening when I arrived, and I waited, as instructed, for someone from Cell Barnes to collect me. It must have been around half an hour later that a green Austin van pulled up outside the station, and a short, slight lad with a gap-toothed smile got out.

'Miss Jordan? Your carriage awaits, miss,' he said with a flourish of his hand towards the van. He took my suitcase, opened the rear door and casually fired it into the back of the van. 'Motton,' he said, introducing himself by pumping my hand. 'You anovver Oirish gel? Which ward you working in then?'

I felt tired and grubby after so many hours of travel. My hair was still full of sea salt from the boat, and my clothes smelt of smoke, soot and smut from the train.

'I don't know what ward I'm in, Motten,' I said, and I realised that I didn't know much about anything. I had no idea what awaited me in this strange country. I had no idea what this hospital was like, and I didn't know what to make of this boy's peculiar accent and his odd name. I'd listened to the BBC at home, but Motten didn't speak like the English people I'd heard on the radio. A lump rose in my throat as I thought, *I know nothing. What am I doing here? I don't even know a thing about nursing.* I realised I'd no idea what I'd let myself in for.

NURSING

My immediate impression of Saint Albans was of a busy town, but I had the growing realisation that Cell Barnes Hospital was out in the middle of nowhere. It was a two-mile drive along quiet country roads before we reached the hospital entrance, and then there was a half-mile-long tree-lined drive through the grounds. Motten was a chatty soul and talked in his unfamiliar accent as he drove. He said he was from Hackney in London but had been working in Cell Barnes' launderette for a year, but I struggled to understand him.

'It ain't no 'oliday camp an' is a bi' quie'er than most ply-says but we 'as our lauffs. We 'as a ree-u lauff some toymes.'

We passed several large buildings before he pulled up outside the original brick farmhouse on the estate. The nurses' residence was in a great red-brick building known as Great Cell Barnes House.

'Fink this is your stop, Miss Jordan,' he said, springing out of the van and dragging my case from the back. 'Alwite? 'Ere's Mary. Her and the gels will show you round now.'

A girl with a bright smile and rosy cheeks had opened the residence door almost as soon as we pulled up.

'Martin, ya big shirker!' she yelled. 'Go lump that case up the stairs for the poor girl.'

I immediately realised two things: she spoke with an Irish accent, and my driver's name was 'Martin' rather than 'Motten'.

'Ger orf yer bleedin' 'igh 'orse, Marie, and do it yerself,' Martin replied good-naturedly before slamming the van door and driving off.

'How are yeh?' the girl said, tugging the battered brown case from my hands. 'Yeh look as though yeh've been dragged through a hedge backwards. Come in and let me show yeh yer room. Yeh poor girl, yeh must be dyin' fer a cup of tay.'

The girl's name was Marie, and she was from Drogheda, County Louth. She was a couple of years younger than me but a year ahead of me in training. I was pleased when she led me to my own room on the first floor. I expected to have to share a dormitory or at least a room with someone else.

'The matron is a holy terror, hai,' she said. 'Yeh need teh keep this place clane as a new pin. She'll be watchin' yeh 'cos yer new, so she will. Make that yon bed and keep that floor clane or, honest teh God, Kathleen, that bloody woman will bate the head of yeh!'

Like everyone's accommodation at Cell Barnes, the room was draughty and shabbily furnished, but it was spacious with high ceilings and a tall paned window. Shared bathrooms were located on every floor. The next day I drew back the curtains and looked out on tilled fields and rolling countryside, half shrouded in a film of early morning mist.

Cell Barnes was originally the site of a nunnery and a monastery before it became a farm estate. The hospital was built as a large and sprawling 'colony for mental defectives' in the 1930s, so it was still regarded as a modern place when I arrived.

In those days, psychiatric institutions in the UK were still operating according to the Mental Deficiency Act of 1913. This act categorised residents into a hierarchy from 'idiot' at the very bottom to 'imbecile' and then to 'the feeble-minded' with 'moral defectives' at the top. All these categories of 'mental defectives' were distinct from 'lunatics', who could recover from their mental illness.

Words like 'idiot', 'imbecile' and 'lunatic' sound so cruel now, don't they, Jade? But people forget they were different times. I can't remember, but I suppose people weren't so easily offended by words back then. They were much harder times, and maybe people had more to think about.

The 1913 Act was considered progressive when introduced because it promoted the setting up of institutions to treat people with intellectual disabilities. Before then, if families didn't care for them, people with mental health problems or disabilities were locked away in prisons and workhouses.

Families often didn't want to care for them because it was considered a terrible social embarrassment to have a relation with mental problems. Parents might find it difficult to marry off their daughters if it became known there was a 'mental defective' in the family.

Things were already changing when I arrived in Cell Barnes. The 1959 Mental Health Act was about to be introduced, and words like 'imbecile' and 'idiot' vanished overnight. It would eventually lead to the scheduled closure of the big mental institutions to be replaced by community care and support for vulnerable people but progress moved at a snail's pace, and Cell Barnes continued to operate for decades afterwards. The hospital was still advertising in national newspapers for nurses years later. When it became no longer acceptable to describe the residents as 'mental defectives', they referred to them as 'the subnormal' in adverts instead.

Cell Barnes was home to around seven hundred residents living within a hundred-acre estate when I arrived. The patients were housed in multiple red-brick buildings or 'ward houses' with men in some, women in others and children from different age groups in the rest.

On my first day, the hospital fitted me for my uniform. The cost of three pinafores, six starched aprons and multiple hats and cuffs were deducted from my salary. I was given very little introductory training for the job and was thrown in the deep end very fast. My first six-week posting was night duty in the infirmary, the medical ward for sick residents.

As a trainee, I had to present myself for inspection at

the matron's office every night, and my uniform had to be immaculate. I had to make sure that even the heels of my shoes gleamed and the seams of my stockings were perfectly straight. Not a stray hair could appear from under my hat. My collar, hat, cuffs and apron had to be starched crisp. We had no rubber gloves back then, so the cuffs and apron were frequently soiled and had to be changed several times a shift. Every shift began with the matron supervising the trainees as we scrubbed our hands and arms to our elbows until they were nearly raw.

Cleanliness was the first, second and third commandment. I don't think there were any cleaners apart from us. We damp dusted every surface during every shift, swabbed the floors and made the beds. When I started, glass syringes, dressings and all equipment had to be boiled and sterilised in stainless steel containers in a big drum and recycled.

The student nurses always got the dirtiest jobs, like being sent to the sluice room to wash out the metal commodes. I was well used to changing nappies and boiling them, so I didn't find it as hard as some trainees. I remember girls who were grey and gagging while trying to complete that task. When I think back, the place was completely understaffed, but I imagine it was no different from any other hospital of its kind at the time.

As student nurses, we were moved around the wards every six weeks at the start, but I remember getting a lot of the night shifts. We trained on the wards, and we studied for our medical and psychiatric exams afterwards.

It was hard work and long hours. We worked twelve-hour shifts, and that was six days a week. It was supposed to be a forty-eight-hour week, but it didn't work like that for student nurses. I found it difficult to sleep during the day with the comings and goings of the day-shift nurses. Loud voices and the sound of slamming doors echoed through the building. I remember feeling utterly exhausted at times.

Resident nurses were provided with regular meals, so we never needed to leave the hospital grounds. There was a strict 10 p.m. curfew anyway, and it was difficult to go anywhere because we were so far from town. Sometimes, girls took short holidays to visit one of their respectable and sometimes fictional 'aunts' in London. In reality, they were going dancing. They loved the Irish dance halls like the Garryowen, the Galtymore and the Blarney on a Saturday night. They didn't go very often because it was hard to get overnight passes from the hospital and even harder to get one that included a Saturday night. The girls had to find accommodation in London too. I remember Marie trying to get me to go with her to London when I arrived first.

'Why not let the oul' hair down for once?' she'd coax. 'All work and no play will drive yeh cracked. Deedin' yeh'll end up as bad as all the rest of the loonies in this place.'

But I didn't drink, I didn't dance, and I didn't fancy the

idea of either. I stayed in the residence and kept myself to myself. I was content to hear all the stories about life outside the hospital when the girls returned from their adventures.

'Yer pure cracked staying in this place all the time,' Mary used to say.

On a few rare occasions, the girls might go to one of the local pubs in Saint Albans, but most of the time, they gathered after lights out to swig bottles of cider that they smuggled into one of their rooms. Drinking never appealed to me, so I never joined them.

I can't say that I ever suffered from homesickness, but I went home to Dublin every chance I got. I didn't go anywhere, so I had the money to get home more often than some other girls. I enjoyed seeing my mother and Joseph again.

Most weeks, I sent Mother a ten-shilling note or postal order. We used to call it 'the remittance'. All the young Irish folk were expected to send back a few bob to their parents in Ireland. Some families depended on it for their survival, but my mother had Daddy's pension, which was a good one. She was better off than most widows. My mother never mentioned the remittance nor expected it, but I always sent it.

Years later, I discovered the money I sent every week rarely arrived. A postman, who worked in the local post office, was caught steaming open mail and pilfering the money. When he saw an envelope from abroad, he knew there was a good chance of cash in it. When I found out, I couldn't believe it. It wasn't always easy to send that money home every week. *God forgive him*, I thought, *what an awful thing to do*. But these days, I think, well, *God love him*. They were hard times, and maybe he needed it more than my mother did.

As a hospital, Cell Barnes was probably not different to other institutions of its size. But compared to today, standards of care and accommodation were poor. Each day revolved around the institution's schedules rather than the residents' needs.

When I first arrived, I noticed a few younger residents who had no teeth at all. I wondered about it because oral health was part of our jobs, and we had to be sure the residents cleaned their teeth. I was shocked when someone told me that their teeth were extracted because they had bitten a member of staff. I don't know if that was true, and if it was, I think that kind of cruelty, pulling out residents' teeth, must have happened before my time. I don't think there was a lot of abuse, but there was probably a lot of neglect.

The food for residents and staff alike was poor. Cooking was done in a central kitchen on the estate, so by the time the food was distributed and served in all the houses, it was often cold and tasteless.

The less disturbed residents were probably exploited too. They worked in all weathers on the big farm estate, which produced much of the hospital's food. This kind of thing was taken for granted, and I don't think anyone ever perceived this as exploiting residents for free labour. The residents didn't have a choice in the matter, but we considered the work therapeutic for them.

We were supposed to schedule all sorts of activities like art and nature projects and dance and music sessions for the residents, but essentials like cleaning took over most of our time. Getting the residents out of bed every morning was another time-consuming activity. Someone hung a sign outside one of the dormitories that read:

Teach us to live that we may dread
Unnecessary time in bed.
Get people up, and we may save
Our patients from an early grave.

Many residents just didn't feel like getting up. The ones who suffered from depression, God love them, just wanted to lie under covers all day. The residents were allowed to wear their own clothes if they had any, but many had no visitors to bring them clothes or money to buy them. They wore hospital garments under an assortment of charity cardigans and jackets. The nurses carried out all activities in the day rooms, reception rooms and dining areas on the ground floors, and patients slept upstairs in big dormitories with about thirty beds in each. As soon as we succeeded in shepherding everyone out of the dormitories, we had to lock the doors or half the residents would be back in their beds five minutes later.

It was the children that I felt sorry for. Some of them were placed in the institution from the time they were infants. Families hospitalised them for various conditions, usually because of Down syndrome or what we know as autism today. Some only had minor learning difficulties and behavioural problems that today would be diagnosed as dyslexia or attention deficit hyperactivity disorder (ADHD). Other children were in there simply because no one wanted them. Their mother or father may have died, and no one in the family wanted to take responsibility for them. That happened a lot then. There were many needy children in the place and never enough staff to devote much time to them.

I saw one little fellow peering out of a cupboard under the stairs one day. When he saw me watching him, he ducked back in and pulled the door shut again.

'Who's the boy in the cupboard?' I asked.

'That's Adam,' a nurse explained. 'Leave him where he is because at least he's not bothering anyone while he's in there.'

But I was curious about the little boy. 'What's wrong with him?'

'Another psychotic.' They referred to children with autism as 'psychotics' then. 'He hits and scratches the other kids and screams the place down when he doesn't get his own way,' the nurse said. 'He's got a horrible temper, and he'll wee all over himself and you if you try to restrain him. He's better off where he is, and so are the other children.'

My heart felt for the little boy in the cupboard under the stairs. It was his own little place where he felt safe.

Adam was twelve years old but was small and slight for his age. He couldn't speak, making loud guttural sounds that were unintelligible. He was an intelligent boy, though, and he appeared to understand everyone around him. Bit by bit, I began to befriend him.

At first, I left toys outside the cupboard door for him. He'd watch through a gap at the top of the door and see me leaving them there. Sometimes, I'd bring him a piece of birthday cake or something he was missing out on by not being part of the class. He never took part in playtime and was never brought outside on walks. The other nurses were adamant. 'He's too disruptive, and he frightens the other children.'

Bit by bit, I coaxed Adam to leave his cupboard so we could play with the toys together. Even if it was just for ten minutes, I tried to make time for him every day. After a while, he agreed to take my hand, and we were able to go outside. He was very nervous at first, but soon his face lit up when I'd extend my hand and invite him for a walk. I discovered a child who was eager to please but was frustrated because he couldn't communicate. He thrived when he had my undivided attention. After a few weeks, I asked the matron if I could let him join the rest of the children. She sighed but reluctantly agreed. 'I don't want him upsetting them,' she warned.

It wasn't all smooth sailing. Within minutes of Adam's arrival into a class, he flew into a fury with another child who had some toy he wanted.

'I told you,' said one of the nurses, shaking her head.

'Give him a chance,' I pleaded.

I took him out of the conflict, hunkered down, held his flailing hands by the wrists and made eye contact. 'No, Adam, you can't hit other children! That's not kind,' I said. 'Do you like being smacked?'

He pulled himself out of my grip, shouted something at me and fled the room to return to his cupboard under the stairs.

I felt bad. *I've pushed things too fast and lost his trust*, I thought. *This will set him back weeks.* But he reappeared at the door later that day, barely able to look at me from under his eyelashes. He was contrite.

'I'm glad you've come back, Adam,' I said. 'We all want you here.'

I brought him to the boy he had attacked. 'Adam is sorry that he hit you,' I explained. 'He won't do it again, will you, Adam?'

But he did, lots of times. And he got smacked plenty of times too. But it happened less and less, and everyone could see the child was making an effort. I enjoyed seeing the transformation, and within months, he was running around outside with the other children, collecting wildflowers and leaves for our nature projects.

Can you imagine how he had felt before that? He saw all the other children going out to play while the adults shouted at him and excluded him. No wonder he lashed out at people. The poor child was only disruptive and violent because he was misunderstood and ignored. Some of the staff marvelled at how he'd turned around. I'd always say that every child is the same at the end of the day: they just want love and attention. They can sense it too if you don't like them. They can sense your anxiety or fear of them.

Because I was so used to being around my brother Joseph, I loved to work with the children with Down syndrome. We had one boy, Billy, an eight-year-old, who couldn't walk. He scooted along the ground on his bum, moving at an incredible pace when he wanted to.

'The doctor says he'll never walk,' Mary told me when I asked about him. But Billy was heavily motivated by food, and I could see he could pull himself into a standing position at the table when he wanted to. I got Mary to help me stand him against a wall for a few minutes at a time each day. It took the two of us holding him because he was terrified of falling.

'We're here, Billy. We promise we won't let you fall,' we had to tell him. As his legs got stronger and his confidence grew, he began standing for longer periods with less support. And then we got him to take his first steps. He kept reverting to pulling himself on the floor out of habit, but after a few months, he began getting around on his feet and soon was able to tear around like any other child. Adam and Billy brought some rare moments of satisfaction in Cell Barnes.

I often think back and remember Celine, an abandoned child who seemed like a little fairy to me. She was so small and fragile, and all smiles and hands outstretched to everyone. She wanted to be picked up and carried and cuddled. You could hand her a flower or a page from a notebook, and she would turn it around and around in wonderment for hours. Maybe she was one of the lucky ones because she was lost in her own happy little world most of the time.

I saw other poor children who treasured dog-eared, sepia-coloured photos of families who never visited. My heart broke for them. They kept hoping that these people would come back for them someday. To this day, I can't understand the kind of people who would do that to one of their own.

Nursing in Cell Barnes could be a rewarding job, but it was often frustrating because there were so many residents and such little time to really care for them. It was heart-rending at times. When I think back, so many people spent their entire lives locked up in that institution, and few people really thought there was anything wrong with that. Some families refused to care for vulnerable family members, so there was no alternative for a long time. I don't understand families like that, but that's what happened.

Cell Barnes continued to operate into the 1990s, before socio-political changes that informed the treatment of people with intellectual disabilities transformed everything. It's sad to think that many of the little children I looked after grew up, grew old and possibly died in that place before the authorities demolished it.

SINGLE

You could see Jean Byrne coming a mile away with her big head of ginger-red curls. Her hair used to drive the matron mad because orange corkscrews sprang out in every direction from under her white cap.

'Kathleen, I'm looking for a flatmate,' she said, sitting down opposite me and smacking her food tray onto the table between us. 'And a little dickie bird said you might be interested.'

Jean always broke the 'no make-up on duty' rule and wore an inch of panstick on her face to hide her freckles. But the matron turned a blind eye that week because Jean was moving on.

To tell the truth, I never wanted to leave the nurses' residence or Cell Barnes. For three years of training and one year as a qualified nurse, I was content with the way things were. I had a big room all to myself and three square meals a day.

The other girls I trained with couldn't wait to leave. A few were leaving nursing altogether because they were getting married, and others had enough of life in a nurses' home in the country. They wanted to live closer to the excitement of London. More and more of the girls I knew were moving out, so things weren't the same any more. I felt torn. I told people I was thinking about leaving too, but I probably would never have left if it hadn't been for Jean.

Jean didn't always get on with the other nurses from Ireland. I can't recall where she was from, but she was a city girl like me. She used to stick her finger down her throat and gag whenever the girls played Irish music like Bridie Gallagher or Larry Cunningham on the record player. Some girls said she was 'stuck up', but Jean was just unusual because she didn't care what people thought of her.

She leaned across the table to me, her eyes wide and restless. 'This flat is great, Kathleen,' she said. 'I've been to see it. It's right in the middle of Walthamstow and close to lots of hospitals, and you can get a job in the morning in Whipps Cross with me if you want.'

But Jean could see I wasn't convinced about moving. 'Oh, come on, Kathleen, even you must be sick of this place. Just think – we'd be living only six or seven miles out from London. It's near the Victoria Line so we could be shopping in Oxford Circus in twenty minutes, or we could go to see a show in the West End at night!'

Her green eyes sparkled at the idea, but I was happy watching *Coronation Street* on the newly installed television in the nurses' lounge. There would be no hope of having our own television in a flat. A seventeen-inch telly cost around sixty or seventy guineas then, and a guinea was a pound and a shilling. Stores charged for luxury goods in guineas then, and a television was too much luxury for any nurse to afford.

Nursing wages were low; one Westminster MP compared nurses' wages to office cleaners', saying we were both paid five shillings an hour. But someone else said it was an unfair comparison because we got five shillings after board and lodgings in the hospital.

My salary as a qualified psychiatric nurse was just over £500 per year or £10 a week in 1961. It wasn't great, but it was a lot higher than earnings in Ireland. Newly qualified nurses working in an Irish mental hospital received £400, and the men earned £435 a year. Men always got paid more than women because it was said they had to provide for a family. I know it sounds strange now, but I don't think we ever questioned it.

Jean pleaded with me to think about moving in with her. 'I'll never be able to afford the flat on my own,' she said. 'But with two of us, it's only two pounds and fifteen shillings each a week, and it's a great place, with two bedrooms. I'll even let you pick the one you want.'

It was only when she mentioned two bedrooms that I began to consider the move. Some of the other girls were happy to share tiny, rundown bedsits in London to save on rent. But a flat with two bedrooms was different. I'd still have my own space, and Jean was a familiar face. Getting work in a hospital was never difficult in those days because most young women gave up their jobs as soon as they married. There was a lot of turnover in hospitals and plenty of vacancies.

In the end, Jean persuaded me to hand in my notice and move to Walthamstow. I got a job, but no, I never got to pick my own bedroom. Jean moved into the room facing onto the bustle of busy Grove Street, but I was just as happy with the quiet room at the back.

We were complete opposites, but we always got along. Jean was an outgoing girl who loved clothes, make-up, shopping and music. The music scene was massive in London in the early sixties, and she went to concerts and shows every chance she got. She cursed her luck at being born with curly red hair and freckles, but she seemed to have a different boyfriend each weekend. Our flat was always busy because Jean brought around many friends and blared Elvis and Billy Fury singles on her portable record player. I remember how she always ran out of money after the weekend. If I didn't keep a few shillings for the gas and electricity meters, we would have been sitting in the dark and cold most of the week. One Saturday afternoon, she arrived home with a man lugging a wooden chest of drawers for her.

'Look what I bought in the market, Kathleen,' she said, slapping the mahogany chest in triumph. 'I knocked her down to five shillings for it!'

Jean introduced the man as Larry Coleman. Tall and lean, he was well-dressed, well-spoken and Jamaican. His skin was a burnished shade between brown and ebony, and his hair was black and tightly cropped. More than a thousand people from the West Indies lived in Walthamstow and nearby Leyton in the early sixties. Jean probably met him in one of her music clubs, but I don't actually remember how they met. When they were leaving our flat shortly after, Larry looked back and hesitated.

'Would you like to come with us, Kathleen?' he said. 'We're going to see this new band in the Bell pub on Forest Road.'

I didn't even have time to answer.

'You're wasting your time,' said Jean. 'Kathleen never goes to pubs or clubs.'

I remember smiling at him. It was nice of him to ask. 'Jean's right,' I said. 'It's not my thing. Thank you anyway.'

And it wasn't my thing. I couldn't think of a worse way of spending my time than in a place filled with cigarette smoke. I still hated cigarette smoke. On many occasions, I'd passed those venues that Jean liked to spend her nights in, and the music was ear-splitting. I'd spent enough time around her friends to know that the smell of beer fumes on someone's breath made me feel queasy too.

Larry became a regular visitor to our flat. He was among a large group of Jean's friends who often called around. He always made sure to invite me to join them if they were going anywhere, but Jean would roll her eyes with impatience. 'She won't go anywhere, Larry. I keep telling you. You may as well give up!'

No, there was no lightning bolt moment between us, Jade. Nothing like that at all. He was just a friend of Jean's, that's all. He was good looking and probably more polite than most of the group she hung around with, but I didn't think much of him. I didn't think about him at all. He was one of many friends who used to call looking for Jean. He was just another visitor to the flat.

Sometimes when Larry called, Jean was out, or she hadn't arrived home from work yet.

'Do you mind if I wait?' he'd ask.

I never minded because he was always polite and helpful. He was handy around the flat and hung pictures for us, fixed leaking taps and things like that. Jean seemed to have him at her beck and call, carrying heavy things up the steep stairs to our second-floor flat. 'Larry's a great guy, and he has a car!' she said with a wink. Jean always thought it was useful to know men with a car.

Then Jean came home from work one day and seemed surprised to see Larry in the flat. 'I told you I was working late!' she said.

'Oh, I must have forgotten,' he said.

Jean's eyes narrowed, and after he left, she said, 'I think our Larry has a crush on you.'

I thought she was mad.

'Well, he always seems to be here these days, and I don't think it's to see me!' She laughed.

Growing up in Dublin, I don't think I ever saw Black or brown people. In London, I saw people of every racial background. London was multicultural even in the early sixties, and after a while, I suppose you don't see people's colour any more. I didn't anyway. I got to know Larry more as the months passed. He would call over, and I'd make him a cup of tea, and he'd talk.

He had a big, bright smile and a deep belly laugh, and he loved his music and motor cars. Larry was passionate about cars and always drove a Rover, which was considered quite posh. Even though he was generally a laidback person, he liked everything to be immaculate. He would pinch a stray crumb off a table and would look around for a cloth if he saw a dusty surface. He was obsessive about cleanliness. *You must have got that from your grandfather, Jade!* Everything had to be neat and tidy, and the interior of his car was always pristine.

Larry was from a mountainous area of Jamaica, about an hour and a half's drive from the capital, Kingston. I remember Larry and I went to the Granada Cinema in Walthamstow to watch the 1962 James Bond movie *Dr No*. I wasn't interested in going to the pictures or in James Bond movies, but I went because it was filmed in Saint Mary Parish, where Larry was born, and he wanted to go. They shot the famous scene where Sean Connery sees Ursula Andress wade from the sea in a white bikini on Dunn's River Falls near where he grew up. Ian Fleming, the author of the James Bond series, lived on the Goldeneye estate close to Larry's childhood home too. I went along with him to see many of the Bond movies after that.

Larry was part of the Windrush generation. He was a youth when he emigrated from Jamaica with his mother around 1950. I think his father had died many years earlier. He had one older brother who emigrated to America, and he never really heard from him again. His mother got sick soon after they arrived in London, and she ended up in hospital for a long time. Larry used to visit her every day until he arrived one afternoon and her bed was empty. The nurses told him she had died the night before. It was sad, really. He was orphaned and alone in England from the time he was sixteen or seventeen years old. I'm not sure how he survived, but I know he worked on the railways first, and by the time I met him, he was working as a bus driver.

He worked the evening service operated by Redline Buses for Hertfordshire County Council and came off the night bus at six o'clock in the morning. He lived in 'digs', as we called them, a room in a family house where meals were included. I remember Larry saying that he fell sick during one of his shifts and came home early one night to find one of the landlady's children asleep in his bed. It was only then he discovered that the mother secretly put her child into his bed as soon as he left for his night shift and removed her before he arrived home in the morning. At least Larry knew the culprit when he ended up with a headful of lice shortly afterwards. The treatments weren't great then, and Larry was a fastidious person. The poor man had to shave off every rib of his hair to get rid of the lice, and the bald look wasn't a fashionable one then.

Our relationship developed gradually. Larry called around to the flat to ask me to see a film sometimes. But I was never really a person for the pictures. I only watched James Bond movies because he liked them. *We never went anywhere in particular, Jade. No, we never went to a restaurant.* After we paid our rent and bills, we didn't even have the money for a fish and chip takeaway. We'd go for a walk in the park, and though he drove for a living, Larry still liked bringing us for a drive on his days off.

I don't remember any colour prejudice in London at that time. No, I really don't. I remember a lot of controversy about Seretse Khama, a Black prince from Botswana, when he married a white English woman. The British government tried to stop the marriage, and his own people exiled him from Botswana for years. But that happened years earlier.

I don't remember anyone looking at us strangely because we were a mixed-race couple. It was just normal to me. Larry and I got on with our lives like all ordinary people. I never saw colour, you know, the way people seem to do nowadays. I don't understand all this stuff, all this racist stuff, in America now. Once I got to know Larry, I just saw a person I loved.

Everyone says there were signs in windows saying 'no Blacks, no Irish, no dogs', but I didn't see them.

The Notting Hill race riots? Was I in England then, Jade? 1958? OK, I was in London then, but I don't remember them. Well, I didn't know any Jamaicans then, so I probably wouldn't have paid any attention to that. Read it to me, so.

[In August 1958, Notting Hill] was gripped by the worst racial violence ever seen in Britain. Notting Hill had been seething with violence all summer. [The riots] started with a minor domestic dispute between a Black [Jamaican] man and his white wife.

By the following evening, a 200-strong mob were rampaging through the streets of Notting Hill armed with weapons, including sticks and butchers' knives, shouting 'Down with the n****rs' and 'Go home you Black bastards'.

'White riot: The week Notting Hill exploded', *Independent*, 29 August 2008

No, I don't remember any of that, Jade. It doesn't ring any bell at all. I probably didn't pay any attention to the news then. Like I said, I never felt prejudice in England.

I wouldn't have experienced anti-Irish feelings because I worked in hospitals, and a lot of the nurses were from Ireland. Many nurses came from the Caribbean too. No, I don't recall Larry getting any abuse either. Nobody cared in the early sixties in London, Jade.

MARRIAGE AND DOMINIQUE

We came out of the registry office on Lea Bridge Road in Leyton into the afternoon sunshine, hand in hand, both of us beaming at one another. I wore a white summer dress. It was just an ordinary dress, not a fancy wedding gown or anything. Larry looked smart as usual in a black suit and white shirt. It's a pity, but there isn't a single photograph of us on the day we married.

Larry and I got married about a year after we first started going out. I think it was September 1963, but I don't remember the exact date. *It was a long time ago, Jade, and I have no documents or anything to check. You know I left all those things behind me years ago.*

We didn't invite a soul. We had to ask two strangers at the registry office to stand in as witnesses. I just didn't want any fuss or wedding reception. That's not me. I can't remember why Jean wasn't there, but I think she must have moved away by then. Larry didn't have any family at all to invite. I don't think he even had an address for his brother in America.

I never invited anyone from my family back in Ireland either. I could have written, but I thought it would be better if I told them myself in person the next time I went home. I didn't have any issues about Larry being Black, but I suppose I must have been nervous about telling everyone in Ireland. Maybe I was naïve, but I couldn't think of any possible barriers ahead of us.

No, Jade, I wouldn't have known that. A white person marrying a Black person was still illegal in America then? I find that hard to believe. No, I didn't realise it continued to be a crime for four more years. I wouldn't have been aware of any of that at all.

It wasn't that I felt like a rebel or a radical or anything. There was none of that. It would never have entered my head. It just wasn't an issue for Larry or me. We were just another couple getting married, and it felt like the most natural thing in the world.

Larry had a circle of Jamaican friends in Walthamstow, but I only met them on a couple of occasions. *No, Jade, I don't recall their reaction to our marriage or Larry saying anything about how they responded.* They weren't unwelcoming or anything, but I didn't have much to do with any of them. I didn't have a lot in common with them, I suppose. To be honest, I never really socialised with them or got to know any of them. Larry kind of did his own thing with his friends, and I kept to myself.

We moved out from the heart of Walthamstow and rented a house in one of those Edwardian terraces on Billet Road in the suburbs. We both worked hard, we had a lovely home, and we were happy. I don't remember us ever really having a row. Larry used to shake his head sometimes and say that I was too quiet. 'How can I fight with you when you never answer me back?' he used to say. I think he thought I was too easy-going sometimes, but that's the way I am.

I preferred a quiet life and never saw the point in fighting with him. He was the same, really. Larry was a mild-mannered man. He'd never raise his voice or anything. There was nothing worth arguing over, as far as we were concerned. If he didn't want to do something, I'd never push it. I'd just do it myself. If I wanted to do something, he'd be fine with it.

A few months after we got married, I decided to visit my mother in Ireland again. It must have been around Christmas 1963.

'I should go with you, you know,' said Larry.

'I think it's better if I tell them I'm married first. It's going to be a big shock for them to hear that, so I'd be better off telling them on my own.'

I still wonder why I got married without writing and telling my mother. I suppose, deep down, I knew what her immediate reaction would be, and I wanted to avoid the rumpus for as long as possible.

Even when I went home, I struggled to find the right moment to tell her. I never wanted to upset her, but I knew she'd be hurt that I hadn't told her. I didn't know what to expect when she heard that my husband wasn't white, but I thought she would come around to the idea after a while. I ended up not telling her until the last minute. We were standing on the station platform at Westland Row, as I was about to leave for London again, when I said, 'Mother, I have something to tell you …'

I don't know what I said. I just remember Mother's face. I don't know how you'd describe it, maybe frozen with shock. But I do remember her exact words: 'We've had our troubles in this family before but nothing as bad as this.' I'm not sure what troubles she was referring to apart from Daddy dying. I didn't get to ask her or say anything else because she turned on her heel and walked away.

Yes, I probably was hurt at the time, Jade, but you know, you get over it. It was a long time ago. I understood, you know. Look, there were ructions in those days even if a Catholic married a Protestant. And no one in Ireland was used to Black people then. My mother probably never saw a Black man in her life. In those days, there were no Black people in Ireland, apart from a few doctors and students training in the College of Surgeons.

It was understandable that the people closest to me would have a bad reaction when I married someone from a different culture. Mother was a traditional Irishwoman, and those were conservative times. *You can't understand, Jade, but I remember the time, and I understood my mother's reaction. I can still understand it.* I felt sure her heart would soften after she had time to think about it or when she had grandchildren.

Our daughter Dominique was born in Thorpe Coombe maternity hospital on Forest Road in Walthamstow in the summer of 1966. She was a beautiful baby, stunning, with big dark eyes and a full head of hair. Oh, everyone admired her. You couldn't help it because she was gorgeous. I called her after my father, whose middle name was Dominick, and the lovely song 'Dominique' by the Singing Nun. The Singing Nun came from a religious order in Belgium, and the song had been a big chart hit only a couple of years earlier. Dominique doesn't like hearing that a nun inspired her name. She doesn't like nuns, you know, but I still think it's a beautiful name.

I stopped working outside the home as soon as Dominque was born. I never wanted anyone else to care for my child, so that was the end of my nursing career. I never went back to it either, and I wouldn't have been different from other women at the time. Larry was mad about our baby, but like most men those days, he didn't do much with her. He'd hand her to me when she threw up or needed feeding and definitely when her nappy needed changing.

I wrote home to let my mother know that she had a new granddaughter, but there was no reply. *Give her time*, I thought. But six weeks after Dominique was born, I received a telegram from my sister Margaret that our younger brother

Jim had been killed. He was in the Royal Air Force and had drowned in an accident in Germany.

God, it was such a shock. It was worse because I hadn't seen him in years. I thought of Jim, Lord rest him, all alone in a foreign country. He had been so full of life and laughter, and now he was lying in a strange place with no one to watch over him. I rang the Royal Air Force station in Coningsby, Lincolnshire, to ask if I could accompany my brother's body home from Germany. After several calls to the base, the RAF responded that they would be transporting my brother's remains in a cargo plane so no family member could accompany him.

Meanwhile, telegrams were flying between our house on Billet Road in Walthamstow and my family home in Dublin. One telegram read: 'Things are bad enough. Don't come home.' I remember my heart sinking and tears in my eyes reading that. I don't really know what was going on in Dublin because then another telegram arrived reading: 'Mother wants you home.'

I didn't care what anyone said. No one was stopping me from going to my brother's funeral. I was breastfeeding, so I never considered leaving the baby for a minute either. I packed my bag, wrapped up Dominique for the journey and left for home. When I got to Holyhead after the long train journey, I discovered that the boat wasn't going because of bad weather. I was delayed in Holyhead for a day, and there was no way of contacting anyone because very few had phones at home then. So when I stepped off the train in Westland Row the following day, I was surprised to see my lovely sister Margaret waiting for me. When I hadn't appeared on the train that morning, she had come back and waited for the evening train.

Margaret was the kindest soul. Straightaway, she reached out to take the baby from my arms, and her face just melted into a smile as she peered into the blankets to see her.

'Isn't she a little angel?' she said. 'She's perfect, Kathleen. So beautiful! It's so lovely to have a ray of sunshine after everything we've been going through.'

I asked how our mother was.

'She's taking it very badly, even worse than we expected. She's taken to the bed and can't deal with any of this at all.'

'Well, I can stay and look after Joseph and help around the house for the next couple of weeks,' I said.

I saw a shadow pass over Margaret's face. 'We thought it would be better if you stayed with me,' she said. 'With the baby and all, it would be quieter. There are so many people calling to Mother's house that the poor little mite wouldn't have a minute's peace.'

I didn't say anything, but I knew immediately I wasn't wanted at home. I stayed with my sister.

No, Jade, my mother never asked to see the baby, but why

would she? After my brother died, she was heartbroken. She had lost her own child, and she wasn't thinking straight. She wouldn't be thinking about a baby, would she? That's what I think anyway.

GOING HOME

When Dominique was a few months old, I came home from the shops in the afternoon and was surprised to see Larry's car parked outside our house.

'What's your daddy doing home in the middle of the day?' I said, lifting Dominique from her pram.

Larry sat at the kitchen table, his head held in his hands, and my heart beat a bit harder.

'What's wrong, Larry?' I asked. 'Are you sick?'

Larry would have to feel really unwell to leave the job early. He rarely took time off work, but he just shook his head.

'There was an accident at work,' he said, finally. 'A child ran out in front of the bus. He came from nowhere. I couldn't stop in time.'

He could hardly bring himself to say anything more, but I asked about the mother.

'She kept screaming. She's probably still screaming, but there was nothing that could be done for him.' He shook his head, but he didn't seem to be able to forget that woman's screams.

The accident affected Larry badly, and I don't think he

ever got over it. *I suppose no one gets over something like that, do they?* I never really heard any more about that day because he couldn't bring himself to talk about it.

Nowadays, people would have some kind of therapy or counselling, but there was nothing like that then. Investigators cleared Larry of any fault, and he went back to work. God love him, I don't think they even changed his route. He didn't have the stomach for driving a bus after that, though. He didn't stick the job for long. You couldn't blame him, with all those bad memories and so many children darting around in residential areas. He packed in his job on the buses and took a new position as a long-distance lorry driver. Larry was away from home a lot after that.

I don't know how to describe Larry as a father, Jade. He was a good father. Who says he was mean? Oh, Dominique ... Well, it depends on what you mean by 'mean'. I suppose you could say that Larry was never easily parted from his money. His obsession was cars, and he spent his money on keeping nice cars. He always drove Rovers, a real luxury brand of motor then. I suppose they must have cost a lot of money.

It didn't bother me. I just made my own money and did whatever I could to keep us all going. We never starved anyway. When I gave up nursing to stay at home with Dominique, I put a notice in a newsagent shop advertising a childminding service at home. Women liked the fact that I was a former nurse, so I could take in as many small children as I could handle. I always liked being around children, and it was great for Dominique because she grew up with children her own age.

When Dominique was a few months old, I saw an advert seeking a foster mother for a newborn Nigerian boy. It sounds strange now that they used to put adverts in the newspaper for children, but they did. They would list any children that were available for fostering or adoption. And the advert would say their parents were from the West Indies, India or Africa, wherever. I suppose that was so people would know they were children of colour. They would advertise their ages too. You just replied to the County Children's Officer or even a box number.

I loved children and babies, and I realised they would pay me to do something I loved. They were offering two pounds a week. It wasn't a lot of money for the twenty-four-hour care of a newborn, seven days a week, but I already had Dominique, and I reckoned I could care for two babies nearly as easily as one.

It all happened far faster than I expected. Someone from social services appeared around a week later with a baby in a small bundle in her arms. She thrust him at me. 'I'm so glad you're home!' she said. 'Yes, it's all a bit last moment, but don't worry, we'll be in touch.' And then she was gone. I remember she handed me a baby in a blanket, and he hadn't a stitch of clothes, no baby bottles, no formula, no nappies. She didn't even ask if I had anything in the house. I don't know if she had any idea that I already had a baby. The woman just handed me a child, bundled up in a blanket, and scurried away.

The baby's name was Ade, a Nigerian name, and it means 'the king' or 'ruler'. It's a name for royalty, and Ade was well suited to the name because he was a gorgeous baby. His skin was ebony, and he had the darkest eyes with long, curling eyelashes. I was mad about him. I had him from the time he was only three weeks old.

I never got to know his mother's circumstances, but I knew that Ade's father was in England, and when the child got older, his father sometimes took him away for weekends.

The house was always full of small children. Dominique and Ade were still babies when our first son, James, was born in our Billet Road home in the summer of 1967. Suddenly, I had three children under two, along with children I minded for other working mothers.

Larry was a real stickler for tidiness; he really was. Nothing could be out of place. Everything had to be dusted and cleaned. Luckily, his job as a long-distance lorry driver meant he wasn't around a lot. Our second son, Jason, was born at home a few years later, in the summer of 1970. My life revolved around caring for small children for years. Money, or the lack of it, was a worry at times, but that was normal life for most people in those days. I did my best to keep those concerns away from the children and to keep us all going. Life was good most of the time, and like I said, we never went hungry. I did my best for all of us, and you know, we managed.

Did Larry ever meet my mother? Let me think, Jade. Yes, he came with me to Ireland on holidays once, I think. Her reaction? Oh, she was grand. Well, she was polite anyway. My mother was a lovely woman and would always be polite. But people on the streets of Dublin stared at him a lot, and I think Larry felt uncomfortable. Yes, I do remember them staring. People could be rude. He didn't come back again for years and years. No, my mother didn't show much interest in the children, and she never really got to know them, which was a pity. But you know, they were different times. They really were, and you had to understand that.

Larry and I were a happy couple. We went around together with our children, and no one bothered us. I suppose I didn't mix much with people in London. Most of my day was taken with looking after the children. I'd have several of them in the pram, a lovely pram from Mothercare lined in navy. I'd bring the children shopping or go to the park on nice days. Other times, I'd sit and watch the television with them. I loved to watch all the lovely children's programmes on the BBC.

You know, I just kept to myself. I had enough to do dealing with four children and minding children daily as well. But I don't remember any racism in England. It's probably because there were so many nationalities over there. Nobody paid any attention.

The only problem I experienced was with our next-door neighbours on Billet Road, and they were Irish people. The wife was always giving us disapproving looks. She would lean against the door, smoking, eyeing us up and down if we were getting out of the car or doing something in the garden or anything. She would never even bid you the time of day, and she used to shout at the children if they made noise in the back garden. I heard her referring to Larry and the kids as 'those darkies' once. I wondered why she didn't move back home if she didn't like people of colour.

Larry continued to be away a lot when the children were growing up. His work took him far away and to every corner of the country. Sometimes, he would come home in the early hours of the morning, but he wouldn't be able to sleep at all in our house. It was too busy with children, so he often had to stay with friends. We didn't see him much. I didn't mind. I liked being with the children, and he had to work, and that was the way it was.

I liked to bring the children back to Ireland for their holidays every year. We always stayed with my sister Margaret. My mother still couldn't get used to the idea of coloured people in the family, I suppose. They were different times, so I do understand, but Margaret and I were always very close. She's the only relative on my side of the family my children got to know when growing up.

Money was always tight, so I never had much in my purse

when I arrived in Ireland. I probably came with twenty pounds and our return tickets for the boat, and that's all I'd have. I counted the pennies, but I wanted the children to have a holiday and know where I came from. They loved it, and I enjoyed going home to catch up with Margaret, and I'd always call to see Mother and Joseph.

I remember how Dominique and the boys used to attract a lot of attention in Ireland when they were small. Margaret's husband worked for Aer Arann in Galway, so she lived in Oranmore in Galway for several years. One day, I was holding Dominique and one of the boys by the hand, looking in a shop window in Eyre Square in Galway, when a woman stopped beside me.

'Aren't they lovely? Are you minding them for someone?' said the woman, looking down at the children.

'Minding them?' I said, confused. 'They're my children.'

'Oh!' she said, startled, and she hurried on without saying another word.

So many people used to come up to me and ask, 'Are they adopted?' Honest to God, imagine asking that? Complete strangers came up to me on the street to ask if my children were adopted. When I told them they were mine, you could see confusion and shock on some people's faces, and you could see the disapproval on others.

It was probably better than the people who would stop and stare at the children. People like that used to make me nervous, and I'd grab the children by the hands and move away. But that was only in Ireland. I'd never get that in England. Really, I didn't, Jade.

But I always appreciated those holidays in Ireland with Margaret. God rest her soul, she died years ago from a brain haemorrhage.

When Ade was about ten years old, I got a letter from social services to say that the fostering was coming to an end. Ade's father was taking him back for good. It happened almost overnight. I'd had him for so long, so it was a terrible wrench for all of us to see him go. I was heartbroken to see him leave.

Ade and Dominique grew up together, so they were like brother and sister. She was distraught when he went away. Ade used to do everything for my older son. He was like a big brother to him, even though there was only a year between them. Ade was mad about him. He fixed his toys and buttoned his shirts and fought his battles. He did everything for him. My boy couldn't even tie a shoelace for himself when Ade left. Afterwards, he was heartbroken. It was a terrible time for all of us. We reunited with Ade years later when he was in his twenties. It was incredible to see him again, and he even moved into our Dublin home for a while.

Maybe a year or two after Ade left, I woke up one day, and it hit me that it was time to leave London. I can't explain what it was that drove me. The idea just came into my head, and it wouldn't go away. It was like the morning I woke and I felt I had to leave Dublin all those years before. I had to move home again. I decided to return to Ireland in April or May 1978. *No, there wasn't any particular reason, Jade. There was no row with Larry. Honestly, there wasn't. My heart was just no longer in London. As I said, I can't explain what it was, but one day I woke up with the feeling that it was time to leave; time to go home. I had to go, and that was it.*

Yes, it might seem daft taking off with three children and moving to a country where I had nowhere to live, but that's what I did. I think it was meant to be. *Can you imagine what would have happened to my poor brother Joseph if I hadn't gone back to Ireland, Jade? Yes, I think it was just meant to be.*

I waited until the kids came home from school one day, and I told them. 'I want you to get ready because we're all going to Ireland at the weekend.'

'Yay!' said the boys.

I could see Dominique's eyes narrow. She was only twelve years old then, but she questioned everything.

'Why all of a sudden?' she said. 'Why aren't we waiting for the summer holidays like we usually do?'

'Would you rather stay here or go to Ireland?'

'Ireland!' the boys chorused.

'How long are we going for? How much do we need to pack?'

I didn't know what to say, so I said, 'Bring whatever you want to carry.'

Yes, Jade, of course I told Larry I was going, and he was very upset about it. He couldn't understand why I was leaving. He never considered moving to Ireland. How could he? He would never have found work there. Oh, I don't remember what he said, or I said, but I know he was very unhappy that I wouldn't change my mind. He said I should think about it for a while, but I had made up my mind. He was so upset that he didn't even offer to bring us to the station that evening.

There were a few things I couldn't bear to leave behind. I packed my transistor radio. And my blanket: a big heavy wool blanket. I bought it from a man who used to travel through Walthamstow with a van selling household things like sheets and blankets and pillows. He'd knock on everyone's door, and people would come out to the road and look at all his wares. Every one bought from him on tick and paid him off by the week. The minute I saw it I knew it was a really good blanket; it has red and cream floral stitching, a tapestry-style throw with fringing all around the edges. Even though it was really heavy and bulky, I folded it up and shoved it into a carrier bag. It was coming with me.

I turned the key in the door that night as we left to catch the boat, and when the kids weren't watching, I threw the key in the letterbox. Oh, I was worried, all right. I had very little money, and I didn't know what we were going to do. I had enough for us to live for a few days in a bed and breakfast in Dublin, but that was all. I hoped I could get a job straight away, but I didn't have a plan. Not a proper one anyway. I looked around at the kids and was glad that they still didn't have a clue that they were never coming back.

Dominique

DUBLIN

The truth began to dawn on me when we were on the train to Holyhead. Mum didn't seem her usual self. She was doing that thing where she looks off into space, and you can nearly see her fretting. She was staring out the train window, totally distracted, cut off from us and the world. And I looked around at our belongings. I had brought my pillow with me. It was my little bit of comfort from home. But Mum had a lot of stuff – far more than she would usually carry. This trip to Ireland was completely out of the blue. We usually talked about it for weeks beforehand, but she had sprung this visit on us suddenly. It was all too quick, so I was suspicious. *What's going on?* I wondered.

I eyed the big blanket. She was always fond of it. To this day, she insists on having it over the end of the bed, and it's a terrible multicoloured flowery-looking thing.

'Why are we bringing that blanket and our radio?' I asked.

'Oh, I just thought we might need them.'

'Why?'

'Well, you never know.'

Mum didn't want to answer any questions. She didn't even want to meet my eyes.

'How long are we going for, Mum?'

'We'll see, Dominique.'

My heart began to beat a bit faster. *Oh God*, I thought. *What are we doing?* Mum was never organised at the best of times. She was always a little bit scatty. I started to worry that whatever we were doing, she hadn't thought it through properly.

'Mum, how long are we staying?'

'Oh, I don't know. I've been thinking that we might stay a bit longer than usual in Ireland.'

'Stay in Ireland? Where?'

Silence. Mum looked out into space as if she didn't hear me.

'Why are we doing this, Mum? What's happened?'

'Nothing's happened, Dominique. What are you worried about? You always love it in Ireland …'

This exchange went round in circles. I couldn't get a straight answer from her about anything on the entire journey. She wouldn't say what happened, and she wouldn't say how long we were going to stay in Ireland. My brothers were upset too. Holidays were fine but they didn't want to *move* to Ireland.

I was always happy to go to Ireland for holidays, even though it was weird for us. People used to stop my mum all the time and quiz her. 'Are they adopted?' they'd say, nodding towards us. Or else they'd be like, 'Is her hair hard to manage?' Or 'Do you have to oil her skin?' Or 'Can I touch her hair?'

'We're not pets!' I always wanted to say. 'I'm not a pet!' But that was not polite. Even as a child, I thought the comments were bizarre and not very polite either.

Still, we always had fun on our holidays in Ireland at Aunty Margaret's. But this was not a holiday. I sensed this trip was something different entirely, and Mum was being very secretive. All my things, everything I owned, was in the house on Billet Road in Walthamstow. My school, my friends, my entire life was in London. Ireland was fine for holidays, but London was my home.

The next morning, we went from the boat to the train, and when we pulled into Westland Row, we began tramping through Dublin city centre. I was tired and in a bad mood. I still hadn't a clue what was happening. We followed Mum down Gardiner Street, down Marlborough Street, back around into O'Connell Street. An easterly wind cut through us, and people eyed us curiously. It was little wonder. We were an unusual troupe – a woman and three Black children carrying our belongings down the main street in Dublin on a spring morning. *What are we doing?* I wondered. The sky was steel grey, and I was freezing. I remember all the dust, litter and dirt blowing around us. I just wanted to go home. I wanted to get back on the train, catch the next boat and go home.

'Where are we going, Mum?'

'We'll see.'

Looking back, it must have been too early to check into a guesthouse, and Mum couldn't afford to bring us into a café to wait. We had to keep wandering until later in the day when Mum could check in somewhere.

In the end, she found a B&B in one of those tall Georgian terraces on Gardiner Street in the city centre. I looked around our room in alarm. It had a lumpy bed, a rusting gas heater and a fluorescent light that highlighted every crack in the smoke-stained ceiling and walls at night. Worst of all, everything looked like it hadn't been properly cleaned in years. God, I hated dirt. I had a mania for cleanliness even then. The next morning, Mum had all these red blotches on her face and neck.

'What's happened to your face, Mum?' I asked.

She looked at her mottled complexion in the mirror, and she looked like she was about to burst into tears. 'It must be from stress,' she said as she gazed at her reflection.

Or from the fleas, I thought, but I didn't say anything because I could see how worried she was. I felt anxious too. Someone needed to take charge, but I didn't know what to do except urge her to get help from another adult.

'Why don't we go to Galway to stay with Aunty Margaret?' I suggested, but Mum seemed to turn a deaf ear to this.

For the next three days, the tension levels rose in our

rented room. Mum counted and recounted every penny in her purse and got quieter and quieter. We followed her around the city, where we sat in beige waiting rooms among rows and rows of people in plastic chairs. We waited for her to be called to a hatch or into a room where she handed over pages of documents to endless officials.

'Why don't we go to Galway to stay with Aunty Margaret?' I asked for the umpteenth time. After all, that's what we normally did when we were in Ireland. We spent two weeks of our summer holidays with Aunty Margaret in Galway every year, and I loved it.

My friends at school in London thought I was mad to be going to Ireland. They believed that I spent my holidays dodging tanks and guns and shootings on the streets. They asked me why I wasn't worried about bombs going off all the time. I couldn't explain what it was like to them. The conflict in Northern Ireland was all they ever heard about the country.

Oranmore in Galway was a hugely different world to London. Aunty Margaret would open the door of her rural cottage in the morning and drive us out. 'Get out from under my feet, all of you!' she'd cry. Together with our cousins and other local kids, we would take off for hours at a time. We'd clamber over stone walls, stalk horses and donkeys in fields and chase down winding lanes to stony beaches. I experienced a way of living that I never did in London. I loved the sense of freedom and adventure for those two weeks.

I figured everything would be OK if we could only go to our Aunty Margaret's place. I knew she would look after us, but Mum couldn't be persuaded; she had other ideas.

'We'll stay in Dublin for a while anyway,' she said.

'But where, Mum? Where are we going to stay? We can't stay in this B&B forever!'

I may have been young, but I sensed how vulnerable we were. I knew from a young age that us kids weren't welcome at Mum's mother's. I never called her my grandmother. She was Mum's mother, but she was nothing to me. She didn't like us, and she didn't want us around.

When my mum's brother died in the Royal Air Force in Germany, Mum was told she could come home for the funeral but not to bring me. Margaret must have told me, or maybe I overheard her and Mum talking about it, but I heard this story when I was about four or five, and it never left me. I often wonder what they thought I was going to do – after all, I was only six weeks old. I can honestly say, even at my age now, this story plays on my mind. To this day, it has a way of making me feel unwanted.

Back then, I wasn't quite sure *why* Mum's mother didn't like us kids, but I was certainly aware that she didn't want us. Anytime we came on holidays to Ireland, my mum would call to visit her, usually just before we went back to England. Even when we were small, we knew we couldn't go into Mum's mother's house. We had to sit on the wall outside and wait for our mum to come out. It was often for a long time. It might have been for an hour, maybe more sometimes, and even though we were kids, we felt it. We felt hurt; we felt degraded. We didn't entirely understand why this was happening, but it felt wrong. Today, Mum prefers to say she doesn't remember any of that, of us waiting on the wall outside, but she does. It's just that she prefers not to think about it.

That's why I couldn't understand why Mum had brought us back to Dublin. There was nothing for her in Dublin, nothing for us.

The days went by, and the contents of Mum's purse dwindled. She kept saying that she was talking to the housing people in Dublin Corporation, and she was sorting out a place for us to stay. I just wished we could go home.

In London, I went to Sydney Chaplin school, a big concrete block of a modern school, on Folly Street in Walthamstow. I wasn't *that* fond of school, but now I longed for it. *Will I ever see my school again?* I wondered. My best friend, Kimberley, lived around the corner. What is Kimberley thinking? Is she wondering where I am? Does she think I kept this all a secret and never told her? I worried that I never had the chance to say goodbye. I had just disappeared off the face of the earth.

Larry? Did I miss my dad? He had nothing to do with us, Jade. I barely knew Larry. We hardly ever saw him. You can't miss someone who's never around, can you? We'd only see him an odd time. It was only ever Mum and us.

I don't know if Larry even knew we were gone. Mum said she'd told him, but I don't know if she did. It was just us and Mum in Dublin. There was no one else we could have turned to.

Then, on day four, Mum returned to the B&B, flushed and breathless. There was a light in her eyes again, and she looked like a weight had been taken off her. 'We have a new flat. They're going to give us the keys tomorrow,' she said.

I was relieved. We had a place to stay. Then I realised getting a flat meant only one thing – we weren't going back to London anytime soon.

SEAN MCDERMOTT STREET

We waited on Sean McDermott Street the next morning, our belongings scattered around us on the pavement. I looked up at the terraces of vast red-brick buildings with peeling sash windows surrounding us. Many of the windows were broken or boarded up. The sashes were raised on some windows, and women sat there watching, occasionally yelling at kids misbehaving on the street below.

I watched as all ages straggled in and out of the huge front doors of these buildings. The doors were wide open, like big maws of darkness, wedged with a rock or broken concrete block. Women struggled out with prams and bawling children. Men with long hair and sideburns cupped their hands to light cigarettes or zipped up their bomber jackets before heading off into their urban surroundings. I didn't understand what a tenement was. *Were all these people sharing one house?* I wondered.

A balding man in an anorak with files of paper stuffed under his arm approached. He glanced from Mum to the three of us. 'Ye're the Jordans?' Mum had never changed her name to Coleman when she married Larry and always says she preferred her own name.

We followed him inside one of the big houses, up a dark and grimy stairwell to a door on the second floor. He turned a key in the lock, but the door was stuck. He put his shoulder to the door and gave it a few hard digs to force it open.

The smell struck us first: damp, mould and something harsh and acrid. But as we wandered in, the darkness overwhelmed us. The main window in the living room was boarded up, and the others were thick with city smog and grime.

Even my mum, who could always put a good face on things, looked a bit shell-shocked. As our eyes adjusted to the dim light, we could see the bare floorboards were honeycombed with ancient woodworm. The plaster was crumbling from the walls and flaking from the ceilings. I opened the door to see a bathroom and instantly recoiled. All I remember was that the toilet was black with God-knows-what filth. For a clean freak like me, that toilet was a nightmare.

The kitchenette at the back had hairy mould that stretched up the walls to the high ceilings. Thick coats of grease covered two dilapidated cabinets, and a door dangled from broken hinges. A filthy gap remained between the cabinets where a cooker should have been. There were two bare bedrooms, just floorboards and crumbling walls.

There was a shocked silence as we gazed at our miserable surroundings. The place was disgusting. This must be hell, I decided. I remember thinking that so clearly: *We've arrived in hell.*

In hindsight, I wasn't far wrong. According to modern historians, Sean McDermott Street and inner-city Dublin contained the worst living conditions in Europe in the seventies and early eighties.

But the man from Dublin Corporation was not sympathetic. He sighed and made it clear he was impatient to leave. 'Missus, this is it; it's all we've got. Take it or leave it, but make up yer mind. I have to go.' He used a nicotine-stained forefinger to tap a page on the top of his file of papers. 'Sign here for the key and the rent agreement. Someone will be along to fix the window and take down the boarding next week.'

I could hardly believe it when Mum took his pen and signed for the flat. I thought we would have been better off on the streets. Mum went off and got some carbolic soap and scrubbing brushes, and we began to clean the place. When it started getting dark outside, we had no option but to sleep because we had no electric light. Mum needed to raise the money for the electricity deposit before the flat could be reconnected.

I was in total despair that first evening as I watched the flat get dark around me. *Mum can't be serious*, I thought. *We can't stay here.* We hadn't even got any furniture.

'We have a lovely house in London,' I argued. 'With a conservatory!' *Surely the conservatory would persuade her? She loves her conservatory. And what about the telly and the comfortable couch we've left behind?* It was Thursday, and usually on Thursdays I watched Jimmy Savile, Tony Blackburn or Noel Edmonds on *Top of the Pops* on the BBC. I couldn't understand this. We had a lovely four-bedroomed house in London. I had my own room with all my things just the way I liked them. Most of my clothes and belongings were still there. But Mum, for whatever reason, had taken us away from our home and brought us to this hovel.

We slept on the bare floorboards, the three of us fighting for the heavy blanket she'd brought to Ireland. Mum used coats and whatever else she could find to make a bed for herself. Eventually, we settled down and started to drop off to sleep. That was when we first heard the scratching.

'What's that?' I hissed.

'Nothing. Go to sleep,' Mum replied.

Then the scratching was joined by squeaking sounds, many squeaking sounds.

'It's just a few mice,' Mum said, but she couldn't hide the panic in her voice. She was absolutely petrified of mice.

Then we heard a fleeting pitter-patter across the floorboards. It had the timbre of something many times heavier than a mouse.

'It's a rat!' I squealed.

'So, what if it's a rat?' said Mum, her voice a higher pitch than normal. 'Sure, doesn't your friend Kimberley have a pet rat?'

'It's a hamster!'

'Same thing.'

'It's not the same thing, Mum!'

It wasn't just one rat: it was many. The whiskered beasts scurried across the floor in the dark. Sometimes even kitten-sized rats would dart across our sleeping forms in the middle of the night.

The lady from across the hall, Mrs McDonald, introduced herself to my mum the next day. 'Lamb of the divine jaysus!' she said, craning her head in the door and glancing around the flat. 'This place is a disgrace. But yer wasting yer breath complaining to the Corpo, love. They refuse to spend a penny here anymore. They keep saying they're going to demolish these flats and build something better, but sure they've been saying that since I've moved in, and that's more than twenty years ago.'

'Is this flat long empty?' Mum asked. 'I can't believe how bad it's got.'

'Must be a year or so now since oul' Mr Cully passed. He was a contrary yoke who wouldn't give you the drippin's off his nose. He kept himself to himself, so God rest his soul, when he died, no one knew for weeks until ...' She thought better of saying any more when she noticed I was listening in on the conversation. 'They locked up the place then, and it hasn't been open since.'

It gave me the chills thinking of a man lying dead in our flat for weeks. *The rats probably ate him*, I thought.

A steady stream of other women followed Mrs McDonald, knocking on the door to introduce themselves.

'Howyeh, I'm Mrs Daly from down the hall ...' 'Do yeh need a hand? I'm Mrs Brennan from upstairs ...' 'Howyeh, I'm Jacinta. I'm just downstairs. If you need anythin', anythin' at all ...'

The kids gathered on the landing behind their mums, tugging at their skirts, eyeing my brothers and me curiously.

'The rats? Oh, those feckers get in everywhere, Mrs Jordan. They come out from under the floorboards ...' Some of the neighbours loaned us some big spring traps that used to snap with a sickening crunch at night. But a carpet of traps laid every night couldn't have kept up with the numbers of furry trespassers in the flat. It's incredible what you get used to. They almost stopped bothering us after a while.

FRIENDS AND NEIGHBOURS

When we first arrived on Sean McDermott Street, I remember standing by the window and watching everything outside. Our house in Walthamstow faced the dog tracks, so apart from passing traffic, we rarely saw anyone from the front window. Sean McDermott Street was a hive of activity in comparison. People were always coming and going, women wheeling prams, kids playing and constant traffic. I was watching, taking in everything.

Everything about Dublin was strange to me in the beginning. I was still astonished by the tenements with their big granite stairs and all the different flats in a single house. But it was the way people would knock on the door for a chat or borrow something that was the most astonishing to me.

'Howyeh, I'm Kitty from below. Yeh wouldn't have a spare drop of milk, and I'll bring it straight back Friday?'

In London, we never had any communication with neighbours. Never. We didn't even know our neighbours by name most of the time. And no one ever *called* to the door unannounced. Not even a close friend would do that without a prearranged invitation.

A few days after we moved in, there was a knock on the door, but this time the callers weren't looking for my mum.

'Howyeh, Mrs Jordan. Is yer young wan coming out?'

I put my head around my mum and saw twin girls my age at the door. I didn't know who they were or that they were referring to me. I'd never heard the phrase 'young wan' before.

'Do yeh want to come out and sit with us?' one of the girls asked me.

Weird, I thought.

'No, thanks,' I said.

In London, I met my friends at school every day or at Girl Guides once a week. Once or twice a year, I might go to Kimberley's house, or she would come to mine, but it was always planned and scheduled. It was different in the flats, where there'd be a rap on the door at any hour and I'd hear, 'Is Dominique comin' out?' This habit of just 'dropping in' was very strange. I never learned to knock on someone's door like that. It was alien to me and still is. It was another week before I agreed to 'play out' with the twins, Yvonne and Angela Gunnery, and we are still great friends today.

Girls would often stand gawking at me as I sat on the step of the tenements. 'Just lookin' at yer hay-yer,' they'd say.

My afro hair seemed to fascinate people in Ireland.

Some of the kids stared; others made to reach for it.

My hair was the big attraction.

'Can we touch it?' they asked, turning their heads this way and that in wonderment.

I sighed. It always depended on my mood whether I'd let anyone touch my hair or not. I wanted to tell them 'fuck off!' But my hair was a talking point. It helped break the ice for me in my new Dublin home. I looked different, and so everyone was inquisitive. But I wasn't a pushover. I wore a hard shell as a child and was never easily intimidated.

No matter where I went, they asked, 'Where are yeh from?'

When they saw my mum and me together, they had more questions.

'So did yer ma adopt yeh?'

'No.'

'Yeh fostered then?'

'No! She's my real mum!'

The reaction was curiosity. The kids found my difference interesting rather than anything else.

Maybe my mum's accent was different or had changed because she'd been in London for so long, but I couldn't make out what people were saying for ages. I was used to London accents, and I was used to my mum and Aunt Margaret's Dublin accents. In the city centre, the accents were stronger than I was used to, and they used different sayings and slang words. I can still remember an exchange with Yvonne and Angela that was lost in translation.

'Isn't it lovely how everyone here asks how you are?' I said.

'What are yeh talkin' about?'

'The way the first thing anyone says is "how are you?"'

'You mean people saying "howayeh"?'

'Yeah.'

'They're not asking how yeh are. They're just saying "hi ya", ya big eejit!'

Ya big Egypt? I was totally confused by now. 'Why do you keep calling me an Egypt when you know I'm from London?'

They would fall around laughing at some of the things I said, and other times they'd ask me to repeat things again and again because they loved my accent. All the girls wanted to know about living in London with its fashion and big shops. The popular TV shows like *Top of the Pops*, *Grange Hill*, *Blake's 7* and *Doctor Who* all came from London. *Jackie* magazine, with all its stories about pop and fashion, was London-based. I told them everything. They couldn't believe that people didn't talk to their neighbours in London, and they couldn't imagine school without religion and Irish classes. They were astonished that I knew boys at school who were gay. Everything was completely different then because London really was another world. The girls wanted to know about the shops, the clothes, the tube, everything about the city.

My brothers and I soon were 'playing out' all the time. We'd first experienced that in our Aunty Margaret's house in Oranmore. But 'playing out' became our new normal. We met other kids in the flats and went out on the streets. Mum had to work a lot. She got work as a cleaner in Switzers department store on Grafton Street very soon after we moved to Dublin. But she used to stand by the big door of the tenement or watch out the window to keep an eye on the boys when she was home.

Only a couple of weeks after we moved in, there was a big commotion on the street. I was sitting outside on the tenement steps when I saw a couple of neighbours running up the road. I realised they were waving up to Mum at the window.

'Quick, Mrs Jordan, yer boy's been hit on the road,' one of the women cried as soon as they were in earshot.

Mum's head disappeared from the window, and she tore past me seconds later. To this day, my mum remembers everything about that incident. She says she was wearing a pair of grey trousers and a pink blouse with a trim of flowers around the neckline. She always says she never wore trousers in her life again after that day because she associates them with Jason's accident.

My younger brother had disappeared out of her eyesight only minutes earlier, and she'd assumed he was around the corner. However, she had to run at breakneck speed to get to Sheriff Street, and she arrived as they were loading him into the ambulance.

We don't know what happened except that a lorry ran

over him. He had many injuries. When Mum returned from Temple Street Hospital that night, she was still trembling and grey with shock. 'Oh, Dominique, he's very, very sick,' she said. She paced the flat, and then she went out to the phone box to call Larry and let him know. The hospital didn't know if he would live or die, and Mum was in a terrible state for days. As soon as the doctors started to think he'd live, they started worrying that he'd lose his leg. The tyres were hot because the driver had been on a long journey from the country, and the rubber melted into his flesh, crushed his leg and sliced off a toe.

Mum blamed herself. 'The lorry could as easily have gone over his head. I could have lost him.' Mum said this to herself over and over again. 'I could have lost him.'

Thankfully, my youngest sibling was stronger than he looked because he recovered. When I was finally allowed to see him, my eyes were out on stalks because his toe was reattached to his foot by what looked like a meat skewer. All the kids were wide-eyed when I told them the gory story of my brother's toe.

Within a short time of moving to Dublin, I knew a wide circle of girls from the area. We would sit on the steps outside the tenements or find a wall somewhere and talk. I don't remember us talking about boys, except maybe to complain about our brothers. We talked about clothes, mostly, because we were obsessed with fashion. All the women of the inner city, old and young, loved their fashion. We talked about platform shoes and wide-legged, high-waisted denims. We watched the young fellas scuttin', which was the term for hanging off the backs of moving lorries, and we watched the comings and goings of people on the street

We didn't do a lot because we never had the money. Some of the kids used to raise a couple of pence to go once a week to Sean McDermott Street swimming pool, but I wouldn't dip a toe in the place. I had a phobia about germs, so no way would I get in a pool used by hundreds of people.

Mostly we went to the shops to try on clothes, even though I wasn't allowed to go into 'town' at first. 'Town is only up the road – we'll just sneak in,' Yvonne and Angela would say. We were all mad about clothes, so we loved going into the shops even though we couldn't afford to buy anything.

Sunday afternoons were special, though, because all the kids from Sean McDermott Street went to a disco in the city centre. It was held every weekend from 3 to 6 p.m. in a place in Temple Bar. This rivalry went on between the northside and the southside kids, and we used to fight each other. That inner-city conflict still goes on today. Around that time, Boney M had a big hit with a song called 'Brown Girl in the Ring'. God, I used to fucking hate it when they played that song because all the southside kids would look at me and nudge each other and laugh. The club played the track week after week. I'd cringe, and sometimes I'd even disappear into the toilets to avoid it. I don't know what it was. I was embarrassed, I suppose. I never wanted to stand out from the rest of the kids. I didn't want to be singled out from the crowd, but this song did that because I was the only 'brown girl' there. Nobody else looked like me in the place. And everyone that age just wants to fit in. They don't want to be made to feel different or like an outsider, but that's how I felt every time they played that song.

It all stopped one Sunday afternoon. There was a particular guy from the northside, a guy that no one messed with. Believe me, it didn't matter if you were a northside or southside kid, everyone knew who he was. People were afraid of him, but I always got on well with the guy. He saw what was going on, and he came over and, in front of everyone, asked me to dance to 'Brown Girl in the Ring'. And that was it. That was the end of all the hassle from the southside kids. Once they saw me dancing to that song with that guy, they didn't dare laugh at me again.

Mum enrolled me in Loreto National School on Hill Street near Sean McDermott Street. It was my first time in an all-girls school, and I was the only girl of colour there. But because I knew so many of the girls before I arrived, I felt accepted. I liked my new school, and I liked my new classmates. The transition to a new school was easy for me.

My brothers were not so fortunate. In Walthamstow, they went to the local school for years without incident. And then they moved to Dublin and found themselves isolated and picked on. Maybe because they were quieter than I was, they were more vulnerable. I think that was because they were good-looking boys and attracted attention from the girls. The other lads didn't like that. The boys would never tell anyone or say anything about being bullied. It was the other girls who told me.

'Yer brothers are getting picked on.'

'No, they're not.'

'They are. There's a gang of lads picking on them.'

'They never said.'

I was angry at the thought of the boys getting grief like this. They were such quiet kids, lovely kids.

'Me brother Donal says they're getting aggro every day.'

'Who's giving them aggro?'

'Tommy and his gang.'

One girl added, 'An' Tommy's sayin' he spat in your sandwiches, and you've eaten his spit!'

'Ugh! That's disgusting. I'd kill anyone who spat in my sandwiches!'

'I know, but that's what Tommy's goin' aroun' sayin.''

'Who's this Tommy? And where can I find him?'

There was no point in telling my mum what was going on. She was too soft, and she is the same today – a lovely person and a real lady without an aggressive bone in her body. I suppose that comes from having a very sheltered background. She was a very loving and nurturing mother, but she didn't understand the rough and tumble of life in the centre of Dublin.

She was also out working a lot of hours, so I felt it was up to me to look after us and run the place. Mum liked a peaceful house. She never wanted any confrontation with her children, so she didn't always set boundaries or limits. I was the bossy one, often making the decisions, setting the rules for my brothers and putting some structure in our lives. I was more responsible than I should have been from a young age. I was a little adult. I set about bringing order and control into our home by ensuring the place was clean and making the dinner. And I was the one who made sure everyone sat down for their dinner. Otherwise, everyone wandered in when it suited them. If there was a problem, I dealt with it. That's the difference between us. Mum tried to ignore things and bury her head in the sand. I dealt with everything head-on.

So as soon as I heard what was going on with Tommy and his gang, I knew it was my job to deal with it. I let everyone know that I was looking for him and that I was going to give him a hiding he'd never forget when I found him. Walking down Marlborough Street with my mum days later, I spotted him.

'You! Come here!' I yelled, and I made to cross the road to get him. He was bigger than me, even though we were around the same age, but to this day, Mum still remembers the sight of the boy turning and fleeing the other way down the street. I must have had a fearsome reputation because he ran like the clappers. He got such a fright that I didn't have to do anything more.

My mum was bewildered by what she saw. 'What are you doing? Why were you after that boy?'

Mum often didn't know what was going on, but that was the end of Tommy and his gang picking on my brothers. But I had to threaten other boys in Tommy's wake to protect them. On one occasion, I threw a punch. Apart from that, I never got in an actual physical fight with anyone. I didn't have to. No one ever messed with me. Even as a kid, I didn't stand for any nonsense.

Larry came over from England a couple of times to see us in the first year or two. I had no connection with him so his reappearance in Ireland for a few brief visits meant little to me, and I have only vague memories of them. My mum will say different, but he was a stranger to us even before we left England. And then we never saw or heard from him again. Mum says things just 'fizzled out'. She was too busy working and looking after us to write or keep any contact, and their relationship just faded away. That's how she explains it anyway.

My abiding memory of the early years in Dublin was the

constant struggle. I swore to myself that I was moving straight back to England as soon as I was old enough or had the money. But it was a financial struggle for everyone. We lived in tenements in the old Monto area of the city like Dubliners had lived for a hundred years before us. The only difference was the landlord during our time was Dublin Corporation rather than the British. Our flat wasn't fit for living in, but most of the tenement dwellers were living in dire conditions. The houses were three hundred years old, and the Corporation hadn't refurbished them since the 1930s. You can imagine how run down they were.

Religion was a very private thing for people in London, but I could see its grip on society in Ireland even as a kid. When Pope John Paul II visited Dublin in 1979, I thought everyone was gone mad. It seemed like the entire country had lost the plot. I remember our street was festooned with yellow and white bunting and banners. Religion was not part of the curriculum when I went to a school in England, and I refused to go to mass with Mum from a young age. Religion didn't rule people's lives in England.

I leaned out the window of our flat and watched thousands moving through Sean McDermott Street in the dark as they headed for the Pope's mass in the Phoenix Park. 'Oh my God, this is weird. It's like zombies out there!' I said.

People were laden down with chairs and big bags filled with flasks and sandwiches and blankets. Mum was packing her own sandwiches and getting ready to join them. She was delighted. 'This is a very special day for the country,' she said. 'Who could ever have imagined that the Pope would come to Ireland?'

I wasn't part of it, and I didn't understand what was going on. *Zombies*, I thought.

SURVIVAL

When I look back, the entire country was in the doldrums then. There was talk of the huge national debt, and the news was filled with strikes, cutbacks and job losses. The people of Dublin's north city centre suffered more than most because the dock work that had sustained thousands of families in the area disappeared in the 1970s. The arrival of heavy machinery and containers on the docks caused more and more redundancies. In the space of a few years, the work once done by forty men could be done by four.

As a result, it was often the women who had to pick up the slack and work hard to keep their families going. Many of them worked long hours and overtime in sewing factories, producing bedding, curtains, home furnishings and clothes.

Following in the footsteps of generations before them, some women earned a modest living as dealers on Moore Street. We'd all hear the racket before dawn as the women manoeuvred their Silver Cross prams down the tenement stairs before walking over a mile to Smithfield market in the dark. On a few Saturday mornings when Moore Street was at its busiest, I'd help on my friends' stalls.

Moore Street was a carnival of colour in those days with the prams and stalls piled high with fruit and veg or flowers or fish. The older women wore headscarves, often tied over their curlers, with ancient woollen coats to keep themselves warm. 'Get the last of the Jaffa oranges,' they cried. 'Five pence a pound the carrots, eight pence a pound the Brussel sprouts.' The butchers on Moore Street were also trying to shout their wares over the clamour. 'The smallest shop on Moore Street for the biggest value – two pound of chops for fifty pence!'

The women made each other laugh and kept their spirits high with jokes and banter. Moore Street was their social life as well as their financial lifeline. The constant stream of browsers, hagglers and complainers was the bane of the dealers' lives.

'The amount of feckin' grief I've had this morning, if Christ was on this stall, he'd be begging for crucifixion.'

'Ya want a refund, do yeh? And I want a bleedin' Ferrari, so it looks like we'll both be disappointed, doesn't it?'

'That oul' rip would only give me 20p for the five oranges, but it's late in the day, so it's better than a kick in the arse.'

Thieving was a constant problem on Moore Street, and the women had to keep an eagle eye out for light-fingered 'shoppers'.

'Young fella, keep yer hands to yerself. Have yeh never heard of forbidden fruit? It's the stuff on me stall!'

Some of the women with prams especially had to be watched.

'Didn't I catch her tryin' to slip a pound of bananas under the babby? And then she sez to me, "I didn't mean any harm, Missus."'

'The cheek of the wan, Annie!'

'I know, Bernie! "That's fine, love," sez I. "And just so you know, there's no harm meant when I reef yer bleedin' hair out!"'

The women spent most of their days commenting on their customers, passers-by and fellow stallholders.

'Would you look at the state of yer wan? Plastered in the slap to get a fella.'

'Yeah, but it's not L'Oreal that wan needs to get a fella, it's Lourdes.'

'If that fella looked any better, I wouldn't be able to help meself.'

'Yer right there, Mary. Ya wouldn't throw him out of bed for eatin' crisps, would yeh?'

Often, their time was devoted to complaining about their husbands.

'I swear, I've no idea how he manages to do so many stupid things in one day.'

'It's probably because he gets up early, Bridie.'

'Is Anto not comin' in with you today?'

'He says he has back trouble. Trouble getting back out of bed!'

And they always had a joke or two to share on the dullest and wettest of days.

'Wait till I tell you, Angie, this woman goes to the priest and sez, "Father, I've terrible news. Me husband passed away last night."

'The priest sez, "Oh, that's terrible, Mary. Did he have any final request?"

'"He did," sez Mary. "He said, 'Mary, put down the bleedin' gun!'"'

The women spent so much time laughing, and I loved to hear them cackling all day in all weathers on Moore Street. I didn't spend a lot of time there, but when I did I saw how the humour and camaraderie of the street kept them going. It was the same for everyone on Sean McDermott Street.

Times were tough in the area, but it's amazing how any situation in life can become normalised. People were broke in the sense that no one had money, but they managed. There was a strong sense of community, and that was a great security blanket for everyone. We were all in it together, and everyone kept an eye out for everyone else. Families and neighbours helped each other, so nobody went without. Nobody slipped through the cracks.

The people had their own welfare system for anyone

who couldn't look after themselves. If anyone was sick, the women got together and organised a rota of cleaners, dinners and childminders. When anyone died, the entire community rallied so that the person would have a 'good' funeral. Parents sat on the steps outside and watched everyone else's children, safe in the knowledge they had full permission to clatter each other's kids when they didn't toe the line.

We were all in and out of each other's flats, borrowing, trading and helping, and everyone knew a woman who could do a job for little or nothing. Mrs Corry was the local seamstress who hemmed all the hand-me-downs for the smaller kids for a few pence. The Dolan family knew someone in Jacob's who sold bags of broken biscuits for a few pence, and there was a woman in the flats who collected all the soft and bruised fruit from the dealers on Moore Street and made marmalade and jams. Several women sat on the steps with their big hot tins of toffee and a pile of apples to sell sticky toffee apples to the kids. All the women exchanged and bartered what little they had. There was a whole micro-economy and huge self-sufficiency around Sean McDermott Street.

Drug addiction was starting to become an issue among the younger generation of the inner city. It wasn't at the epidemic levels that it reached a few years later. Crime levels began to rise in the area because the kids had to fund their £10 heroin deals from somewhere. Youths began snatching handbags and jackets from cars at traffic lights in the area, often flinging a dead rat in the window as a diversion.

All the parents were worried because no one wanted a child involved in drugs. Mum would have died if any of her kids had been caught up in crime. She was like most of the others in the tenements, law-abiding people who were never in trouble in their lives. But at that stage, the scourge of drugs was only affecting the unlucky few.

We were so lucky to have had the best of neighbours, who we are still friends with today, like the Gunnerys, the O'Connors and the Lambs. The people of the city centre were the best people you could meet: honest, hard-working and decent. They were the best friends you could have. Despite all the challenges they faced, the spirit of friendship in Sean McDermott Street was incredible. People were poor in their pockets and purses, but they were rich in character and heart. It was the first time I'd ever experienced that great sense of care in the community. I think it was starting to dawn on me that there was nothing like it in London.

One of my mum's relatives also lived in the heart of the city centre. We called her Aunty Fan, but her real name was Frances, and she was my mum's aunt and our great-aunt. She was a real lady, a kind-hearted soul who never had much, but anything she had, she would give it away. She lived in nearby Ballybough, and as soon as she heard we were in Dublin, she came looking for us.

'I wish I hadda known sooner that youse were back in Dublin,' she always said. She said we could have stayed with her until we got back on our feet. This kindness came from a woman who shared a house with her daughter and thirteen grandchildren. Yet, she wouldn't have hesitated to invite four more of us under her roof.

The people of the city centre embraced our unique family and accepted us all. They asked a few questions like 'Are youse adopted?' and 'Where are yeh really from?' but they were just curious, never disapproving or judgemental.

The first time I experienced a racist comment from a stranger happened after 'the boat people' from Vietnam arrived in 1979. There was a lot of hostility and anger that the government was 'bringing in immigrants' when many Irish people were poor and homeless. Hostility levels against anyone who happened to look 'foreign' rose in the wake of that controversy. The first time a racist incident happened to me, it came out of nowhere.

I was on my way home from secondary school, Parnell Tech. A man in his thirties or forties, old enough to know better, stepped in front of me on the road, glaring at me. I don't remember his exact words, but he said something like,

'We don't want *your kind* around here. Go back to where you came from.'

I stared at him in astonishment. 'What did you say?' I said.

'Go back to where you came from,' he hissed.

I was a year or so in Dublin at that stage and knew by his accent that he was a person referred to as 'a culchie'. Even though his eyes bored into mine with pure hatred, I took another step, right up to him. 'I come from Sean McDermott Street in Dublin,' I said. 'Why don't you fuck off back to whatever bog you came from?'

I never thought I'd hear myself say that. *I come from Sean McDermott Street*. But I said it with pride and defiance because I felt part of a community, a real community. And I was very proud to be part of it.

BLANCHARDSTOWN AND SCHOOL

The bulldozers started moving down through Summerhill, Gardiner Street, Foley Street and Sean McDermott Street in late 1980 and early 1981. We could hear the rumble of machinery and the crash and thud of collapsing buildings as they approached. Layers of dust from the sites covered every surface. The Corpo had boarded up many tenement windows, and thousands were on the move out of the city centre.

It was bittersweet for many. There was some excitement because families were getting new properties with gleaming kitchens and proper heat and plumbing for the first time in their lives. But the entire community was splintering, and generations of families were being torn apart, allocated homes across different parts of Dublin. Only a few who had the strongest, longest roots in the city centre got to stay in new accommodation in the area. Most people had to move out of the inner city. There was a sense of upheaval, bereavement and loss too.

I was a teenager who had already been uprooted from London, and now we were on the move again. I was happy in Parnell Tech, my new secondary school, so I felt like my world was being shattered again. Sean McDermott Street had become a home for us, a place where I now felt we truly belonged, and the prospect of starting over somewhere else, leaving a life I'd grown to love behind once again, filled me with intense sadness and fear.

Like all teenagers, I was going through something of an identity crisis, but my identity crisis was a bit more confused than most. Back in London, Larry sometimes brought us along to parties and events at some of his friends' houses. The Jamaicans loved to gather in big, boisterous groups, but they were stand-offish around us. The women never pulled us into their bosoms the way they did to the other kids. Even though I was young, I knew Larry's Jamaican friends never really accepted us.

'My dad says you're mongrels,' one of the Black kids told us.

I remember that well.

'Mongrels?' I said, having no idea what that meant.

'You're not proper Blacks,' he said. 'You're mongrels.'

I suppose mixed-race marriages must have been a big deal in the Black community too in the 1970s. They saw Larry going off with a white woman and having three children with her. They probably weren't happy about that either. Prejudice comes in many forms and colourism is one of them; seemingly we weren't Black enough to be accepted into the Afro-Caribbean community at that time. Even though Larry was part of that vibrant Jamaican community in London, Mum was alienated from that side of his life. I don't remember my mum ever being invited to any of the Jamaican events.

In England, my dad's community ostracised us because we weren't Black enough. In Ireland, we had people who didn't want to know us because we weren't white enough.

At least in London I could blend in with the many shades of Black and brown people. But when I moved to Dublin, I stood out because there were no other ethnicities around then. My skin was far darker and my hair was far curlier than everyone else's. No one seemed to believe that my mum was my real mum. When people asked 'Where are you from?' I used to say 'London' and hope that would be an end to it. Usually, it wasn't. 'But where are you *really* from?' they'd ask. I began to question it myself. I didn't seem to belong anywhere. Is it any wonder I had an identity crisis?

Dublin Corporation gave Mum a choice of three new or newish properties, the first of which was a house around the old cattle market off the North Circular Road. We went to have a look at the place. It was in a square of red-brick houses, and to my young eyes, it seemed walled-up, and everyone seemed to be looking into everyone else's homes. I was glad that Mum didn't like it much either.

We were also offered a place in a new development in Tallaght, but Mum didn't want to accept it because she heard that it took two days to travel all the way out there.

Remember, this was nearly twenty-five years before the Luas was constructed. Many families were reluctant to move from the centre city to Tallaght because everyone thought it was in the middle of the country.

'I told the Corpo they could ask me arse,' Mr Ryan said. 'Tallaght? Sure you'd get to America faster.'

So, Mum accepted the third option: a three-bedroomed house in Fortlawn Park in Blanchardstown, even though we didn't know what the area was like.

I can remember the day we got the keys and went to see our new house for the very first time. There was only one bus route, and it was an hourly service, so we had to wait for ages in the winter cold. Once we boarded the bus, the journey seemed to go on and on. The further we went from the city, the further my heart sank. Houses and shops gradually thinned out and began to be replaced by fields, hedgerows and wilderness.

Fortlawn Park was then a row of newly built homes in the middle of the countryside. It was the middle of nowhere for me. I hated our new area and our new house on sight. I hated everything about it. I never fully appreciated Dublin's city centre until that day. Then I realised that I definitely didn't want to leave Sean McDermott Street. Blanchardstown, back in December 1980, was a teenager's worst nightmare. It was remote, isolated and rural.

'There's nothing here, Mum!' I cried. 'This place is a dump!'

But my mum was enchanted by the newly built house, clean and immaculate, set on a small patch of rubble, which could soon become a garden. For me, Blanchardstown was hell. I would have done anything to stay in the flats, but the entire terrace was about to be demolished. The bulldozers were lined up, and all our neighbours and friends were already leaving. We were moving to Blanchardstown, and that was that.

Mum hoped to get a place for me in the local school. Attending Parnell Tech in town was no longer an option once we moved to Fortlawn Park. There was no motorway then, and with the bus travelling up and down every laneway, it took two hours to get to the city centre.

It was the middle of the school term when my mum and I went up to our nearest school. The person we approached was adamant there was no place in the school for me. Mum was understanding because she knew the school year was already well underway.

'What about her starting in the school next September?' she asked hopefully.

'You're new to this area, and other families have priority. We have a long list of applicants, so there is no chance of getting in,' they said.

Mum was very disappointed. She didn't know what she was going to do about getting me into a local school.

By now, many new families were moving into Fortlawn

Park, and we were starting to meet our new neighbours. Like us, many of them were from the city centre but came from other streets and tenements. Mum was happy because it felt like a new community coming together. By pure coincidence, we met a family with a girl the same age as me and discovered that the school had accepted her *after* turning me down. Mum was upset when she heard about this.

'They only went up to the school on Friday, and their girl was given a place. We were there the Monday before her, and they said they were full. How can that be?' she asked over and over.

Mum rarely gets angry or worked up about anything, but she was determined the school would not get away with this. She returned for another meeting.

'My daughter was here with me last Monday, and you told us there was no place for her here,' she said. 'In fact, you told me that she would never get in. But I've been told that a girl from around the corner came here on Friday and was offered a place straight away. Are you discriminating against my child because of her colour?'

They hadn't counted on all the families in the area talking to one another. They realised they hadn't a leg to stand on once they'd accepted the other girl on the road after me. Needless to say, I got my place in the school, but they gave it grudgingly, and I was made to feel very unwanted.

Over the next few years, I paid a heavy price for my mum being 'troublesome' and demanding that I get a place in the school. I encountered several nasty people there, and none of them were pupils.

It was difficult arriving in the middle of second year when everyone had already formed their own friendships and cliques. I was at that age when I wanted to blend in rather than stand out. That was hard when I was the only girl of colour in the school. I also still had an English twang to my accent, and I was called Dominique when most girls were called Bridget, Ann or Mary. Lots of the kids couldn't even pronounce my name and called me 'Domo' instead, which made me sound like a boy. My mum used to hate it. I remember one girl arriving at the door and making the mistake of asking for 'Domo'. 'No one of that name lives here,' said Mum and then shut the door in her face.

It was a mixed school, but the children there were never a problem. It was several of the supposed 'grown-ups' who made my life a misery. The Catholic Church was still heavily involved in the administration and teaching at the school. We had an elderly sister for religion, and from the first day I appeared in the classroom, she picked on me.

'Oh, the new girl is here!' she said like she was waiting for me. She peered over her spectacles and down her nose at me. 'Well, this is a chance to let us all see how much you know. Stand up now, and tell the class all you know about the Second Vatican Council.'

Needless to say, I knew nothing about the Second Vatican Council – or any other Vatican Council, for that matter. But she achieved her aim, which was to humiliate me in front of a classroom full of strangers on my first day. I was still new to religious education, and our mum didn't force us to be part of any religious tradition. I knew nothing about the subject, and the nun used every opportunity to showcase my ignorance.

The girls in the class were kind, though. 'Don't pay any attention to her,' said one. 'She's an awful oul' bat. She's never happier than when she's picking on someone, and this week it's you.'

But it wasn't just that week. Everything about me seemed to infuriate her. Perhaps it was because my mum had accused the school of racism or because I knew nothing about religion. But I felt there was more to it than that because that nun held a real disgust for me. Religious education is supposed to promote tolerance, mutual understanding and respect for other cultures and beliefs and even non-believers. But tolerance and respect mustn't have been part of the religious curriculum in the early 1980s.

I loved school apart from that nun and a couple of other teachers. The girls were great. Soon I had a strong and supportive bunch of friends who made me laugh all the time.

'You know, we could put out a hit on Sister Hitler.'

'I say we wait. She must be nearly a hundred. She has to die of old age soon.'

'Or a stroke. Did you see the purple face on her today? Jayz, Domo, you'll be a legend if she drops dead yelling at you.'

'To hell with her, why don't we just go on the mitch?' I remember a girl suggesting before religion class one day.

'On the mitch' was one of the many new phrases I had to learn after moving to Dublin. But I never went on the mitch. I loved learning, and I loved being at school, and even though I was tempted to skip religion class that day, I didn't take up her offer. I was determined that nun was not going to bully me out of the class. But everyone knew what would happen once class started.

'Well, Dominique, would you share some of your brilliance with the class and answer?' 'Do you plan to get anywhere in life, Dominique, or are you happy with your empty head?' 'Why don't we ask the brain of Britain, girls? Dominque, stand up and give me the answer.'

It was twisted, vicious, prolonged psychological abuse. She would prod me in the back with a bony finger and startle me by banging a book on my desk. For more than a year and a half, she belittled me.

Some of the girls even risked their necks by trying to intervene.

'Sister, you're not even giving her the chance to answer.'
'Sister, stop picking on her. None of us knows the answer.'

The girls insisted that I should get my mother involved, but I didn't want to worry her. I reckoned I could handle anything that nun threw at me. I was confused by it all because I wasn't a bad kid, but it seemed like my presence revolted this woman. That nun was determined to torture me every class, and I was equally determined she wouldn't break me.

I look back on what happened now, and I still don't understand it. I certainly experienced unwanted special attention from that nun. That attention meant that I felt almost physically ill going through those school gates every morning. The anxiety that I experienced was enormous. I wasn't a problem student. I wasn't disruptive in class. Unlike a lot of kids my age, I never drank, and I never smoked. The most I would do is give back a bit of cheek, but I never caused trouble for my mum or the school.

The pressure in her classroom built and built until something had to give. I was in my second year or so there when the nun humiliated me one too many times. She asked me a question, I can't even remember what it was.

'Well?' she said. 'I'm waiting.' She pursed her lips with disdain, and the whole class seemed to hold a collective breath. 'Has the cat got your tongue, stupid girl?' She spat the words at me.

My heart thumped, my stomach churned, and my eyes

stung, but I was determined not to cry. I would never give her the satisfaction. I felt this deep well of anger bubbling up within me.

'We have gone over this so many times, but you are such a stupid, stupid girl. I don't know why I have to waste my time on the likes of you. You're not fit to be in this class. You are a disgrace. What are you? Stupid! Stupid is what you—'

That's when I screamed, really screamed, and I picked up my chair and flung it at her with every ounce of strength I had. The satisfaction of seeing her cower with fright overwhelmed me. I heard the entire class erupt in laughter as I ran out of the room. I only remember being sure about one thing: that nun got what she deserved.

JOSEPH

It was all a bit mad after that. Several teachers heard the ruckus and came running, and I was escorted off the school premises. I was dragged by my school jumper, to be more exact, and thrown out the school gates. They officially expelled me from school after that and were happy to have the excuse to remove me.

Mum knew I was having trouble with the nun, so once she got over the shock of what I'd done, she was upset for me rather than angry with me. 'Maybe it's for the best, Dominique. They never wanted you there, so maybe you're better off out of there.'

But I was stunned. *What am I going to do now?* I thought. No one ever *made* me go to school. My mother didn't push me through the gates every morning. It was *me* who wanted to be in school. I was the one who wanted to learn, and now it was over for me. I knew it would be nearly impossible to get into another school.

I didn't feel any remorse over flinging a chair at the nun. I despised her, but it felt like I had let her win. She had never wanted me in her class or in that school, and now she had her way. School was finished for me, and I felt lost. This was not where I intended to be when I was fifteen years old.

A couple of the girls called to see me later that week. They felt my expulsion was unfair, and they were angry that the nun was being seen as an innocent victim. Everyone in the class knew there was far more to the story.

'Look, don't worry, Dominique, this is not over,' said one girl. 'Everyone knows this is unfair.'

But I was convinced that my school days were finished, even when the girls told me that some students and parents objected to my expulsion.

'My mum is annoyed,' said another. 'She knows what's been going on. She says she's going to have words with the principal.'

'We were talking about it in the class today, and the guys said the same thing,' a girl said. 'They said their parents want to talk to the principal too.'

I couldn't believe that even some of the boys in the class were standing up for me.

'Everyone knows what was going on,' said another. 'My mum said something should have been done about that nun ages ago. She's been out of control for a long time.'

I don't know how many parents approached the principal in the end, but there were enough representations on my behalf to make the principal back down. Parents said they were alarmed by what they heard had been happening in the classroom. They said they believed I had been victimised, harassed and provoked by the nun. They also said that the sister's fitness to teach needed to be questioned. I heard all this from the girls. There were meetings and more meetings until, a week or so later, they decided to quietly readmit me to the school.

For years I had sat in the library on my own during Irish classes. Nobody had explained to me that I was considered too old to start Irish when I moved to Dublin. I was told I wasn't wanted in Irish class. *Stay away. Go sit in the library.* No one ever offered an alternative. After I was readmitted, the school decided I should also sit in the library for every religion class. I was isolated. I felt like an outcast, sitting on my own every day while school went on as normal for everyone else, so it still felt like I was being punished. Looking back now, I know that no child should be treated like that.

The constant abuse came to an end, though, because from then on, it was as if I was invisible. The hostility was still there, but no one yelled at me or abused me again. Still, I think the damage was done by then, and I kind of lost heart in school. For the first time in my life I went on the mitch. I lied about my age and got a job on a conveyor belt in a factory for a few months, but I did go back to school.

There was only one student who upset me during this time. And it wasn't his fault – he only listened to an adult. I asked around for a loan of a pen one day. It was just an innocent request, but this fella turned around and said, 'Don't give her a pen! She could have AIDS!'

I was stunned. My friend Jackie looked at me because I always had a smart answer on the tip of my tongue, but this time I had nothing.

'What are you talking about?' I said to the boy.

This was the early 1980s, and we'd all heard about this new 'killer disease', but we knew nothing about it. There was only terrible fear and stigma surrounding it.

One of the other fellas said, 'You can't say that. She doesn't have AIDS.'

But the boy was adamant. 'Me da says this disease comes from gay people and Black people.'

I didn't answer him. I didn't know what to say. Jackie looked at me afterwards and said, 'You didn't have a comeback!'

'That's because I don't know anything about AIDS.'

For all I knew, that boy could have been telling the truth.

I went home and asked my mum: 'Do all Black people have AIDS?'

'No, Dominique, of course not, but I don't know much about it.'

I started asking people about it – it wasn't like I could just go and Google it because there was no internet. There weren't even any books about AIDS then. I talked to as many people as I could, and I went back to the fella four or five days later and said, 'You can tell your uneducated father that all Black people don't have AIDS, and it's a disease that anyone can get.' But that was what it was like then. Young people were afraid because they thought you could even get it from kissing.

While I was still in secondary school, Mum's mother died of a brain haemorrhage. Mum went to the funeral, but we, the grandchildren, weren't invited. Mum's mother's decisions had to be respected, even after her death.

The day after her funeral, Mum insisted on us all going to her mother's grave together. I was outraged, but I knew my mum was grieving, so I went along even though every fibre in my body was indignant.

I stood with Mum looking at a mound of clay in Glasnevin Cemetery. I sighed in exasperation. 'What are we doing here, Mum?'

'You are paying your respects to your grandmother.'

'I don't have any respects to pay to her.'

I remember looking at a pile of earth, a filled-in hole in the ground. I couldn't understand why Mum would insist on us being there. She even took a photo of her three children looking blankly at the grave. I was bored and irritated. I didn't know her mother, and she hadn't wanted to know me, so this was plain weird as far as I was concerned. I had no feelings for the woman one way or another. I didn't hate her, but I didn't care about her. The truth of it is she was a stranger to me.

No, I wasn't offended that I hadn't been asked to the funeral, Jade. I didn't care because she didn't mean anything to me. I was probably more offended that Mum made us go to the grave the next day. That offended me more than anything.

I couldn't understand why Mum had put up with how her mother treated us all our lives. My mum had always been told her father intended to leave her the family house. I often wondered about her father and if he saw a kindred spirit in his daughter Kathleen. Maybe he knew that she would always care for her brother Joseph. My mum saw how her mother treated us, her children. Yet, to this day, she won't hear a bad word said about her mother, and it can drive me mad.

'Mum, please stop trying to tell me that she was a lovely woman!' I'm forever saying. Seriously, who disowns their own grandchildren? Who would do that? I can't imagine, but Mum won't hear of it.

There's one story about my mum and her mother that makes me smile, though. When my mum was very young, she had to bring a penny into school every week for 'the Black babies'. Collecting money for 'the Black babies' was a regular thing in the religious-run schools then. But Mum came home from school one day, after about a year or so of bringing in her pennies, and she was very upset.

'I brought in all my pennies like I was told,' she wailed to her mother, 'but they're not giving me a Black baby!' For some reason, she had believed that she would get a baby at the end of all her efforts. Her sister Margaret remembered the story from childhood, and she and I used to joke with Mum about it. 'Aren't you a lucky woman that you ended up with *three* Black babies?' we used to laugh.

I may have had lots of relatives, but I didn't know them when I arrived in Ireland. Instead, I found lots of good friends, especially from the time we moved to Blanchardstown. I was different, but it never really mattered because I felt accepted by my peers. My afro hair and dark skin were admired and even envied by some girls around me. Hair styles were big then, and so was my afro. The other girls had the Farrah flick in their hair, modelled on Farrah Fawcett, or a version of the mullet or mohawk. They went to Peter Mark salons for styling, while I depended on my mother to cut my hair. No hairdressers in Dublin knew how to work on my hair. It didn't matter because I always felt like one of the girls as a teenager. However, the boys still didn't accept my brothers, even as they grew older.

One day, I heard that one of my siblings was being picked on again.

'Who's doing it? Whose picking on him?'

'Tommy Ellis.'

I knew the family. My mum was friendly with his mother. I didn't know Tommy, but I knew the Ellis family lived not far down the road.

'Are you sure?'

'Yeah, it's Tommy Ellis.'

The next day, I walked down to his house and knocked on the door. His mum answered.

'Hi, Mrs Ellis. Is Tommy there, please?'

'Oh, hi, Dominique. How's your mother? Hold on. *Tommy! Someone at the door for you.*'

Tommy came to the door, but he didn't even have time to say 'hi' because I punched him square in the face. Hard. With closed knuckles. He staggered back into his hall, holding his face.

'There's more where that came from if you try picking on any of us again,' I said, and I turned on my heel and marched home again.

It was only about a fortnight later when I heard my mum shout, '*Dominique? Someone at the door for you!*'

I looked out and saw Tommy standing there, so I braced myself. *So, he's come to punch me back*, I decided. *Well, I won't make it easy for him.* I rolled my fist into a tight ball and got ready to hit him again.

But Tommy beamed a big friendly smile instead. 'There's a gang of us going to Blanchardstown disco this weekend. Do you want to come with us?'

'Really?' I was suspicious.

'Yeah'.

I shrugged. 'OK.'

I joined a gang of kids in the area that Saturday night, and we all went to the local disco together. It wasn't a boyfriend–

girlfriend thing. It was just a group of us having a laugh, and I became part of a new circle of friends. Tommy never picked on my brothers again, and he and I remain friends. We still laugh today about how we met. How many can say that they were introduced by a punch to the face? Many years later, I asked him, 'Why did you do that? Why did you want to be friends after I did that to you?'

'I suppose I had respect for you,' he said. 'I knew I deserved that dig, and you didn't let me away with it.'

I was lucky in that sense. I was a real tomboy who was well able to stand up for myself.

When we lived in Fortlawn, Mum got up early most mornings. She was often getting meals ready or cleaning the kitchen before dawn, and one morning, someone or something rapped hard on the kitchen door. She leapt with fright because it was around 5 a.m., still dark, and no one else in the house was up. She opened the kitchen door, looked into our hall, but no one was there. She wondered if she'd imagined it, but her thumping heart told her otherwise.

The next morning, the same thing happened again, and she was spooked this time. The hair rose on the back of her neck as she opened the door, knowing she would see nothing on the other side. The knocking happened the next morning and the morning after. She never said anything to us in case it made us nervous. It was only much later that one of my brothers admitted he heard it too because it used to wake him. He wondered why Mum was banging on the door.

Then one day, I came home from school and found Mum in a terrible state. She was pacing the kitchen and had two bright-red spots on her cheeks. Her mother wasn't long dead at this stage.

'I've just heard poor Joseph is in Portrane mental hospital,' she said. Joseph had lived all his life in the family home with his mother. 'He's locked up in that awful place, and I never knew.'

Mum had been a patient in a psychiatric hospital and had worked for years in another one. There was no way she was going to leave her brother languishing in any institution. Her greatest concern was how she was going to get him released into her care. 'Whoever put him in there is the only one who has the power to take him out again,' everyone told her.

Mum caught the bus to St Ita's mental hospital in Portrane the next day, Friday, 9 April 1982. She told us afterwards that she walked around the big red-brick building and spotted Joseph through a window.

'Lally!' he cried when he saw her. He jumped up and down and waved in delight. 'Lally! Lally! Lally!' He always called her Lally for some reason. She went inside and told the staff she was taking Joseph out for the weekend. She found his anorak, took him by the hand and left with him.

'He never went back into that place, and they never looked for him either,' she always says.

I had just dyed one half of my hair shocking pink and the other half bright green when Mum arrived home with Joseph. I always had this rebellious streak in me and took great delight in madly colouring my hair that day. It must have looked crazy because Mum noticed. Her mouth dropped open as she saw me. Joseph took his new surroundings in his stride and hardly gave me a second glance before running up the stairs.

'What did you do to your hair?' Mum asked.

'Look at Uncle Joseph – he's not bothered about it,' I said.

Mum was about to follow Joseph upstairs when he started thumping down again. He had been wearing a straitjacket when she found him in Portrane. It wasn't tied, but it was still a straitjacket, and Mum was also upset because she'd found him unshaven. She always said he didn't look cared for when she found him. Joseph handed her a cream garment scrunched into a ball when he got to the bottom of the stairs. 'Lally!' he said.

She opened it to discover a wool vest. Mum's mother battled all her life to get Joseph to wear a vest, but he refused. Somehow, the hospital had managed to get one on him, but the minute he regained his freedom, it was the vest, not the straitjacket, that had to come off!

Mum still swears that the day Joseph walked through the

hall door was the day that the knocking on the kitchen door stopped. 'I know it was my mother,' she always says. 'She was trying to get through to me about Joseph. She would never have wanted him to be put away like that.'

She also says Joseph must have been the reason that she felt compelled to return from England. 'Something was telling me I had to come home,' she said. 'And sure, within a couple of years of me coming home, my mother died, and Joseph was put away. What would have happened to poor Joseph if I wasn't at home? I was meant to come home; I really was.'

That's her explanation now for why she brought us to Ireland as she did. And if there ever was another reason, I'm not likely to find out now.

FAMILY

'Love the afro!'

A man stood across the street with a boyish grin and a mischievous sparkle in his eyes. He looked vaguely familiar. I thought I'd seen him around the area before.

My hair was big, abundant and defiant, so it was sometimes the object of ridicule. I was immediately on the defence.

'Shut up, you!' I replied. 'Anyway, you could be my da. You've got an afro yourself!'

And he did have an afro. He had the pasty white complexion of any Irishman, but he had those kinky, tight curls.

'Gerrup outtadat, yeh cheeky bugger,' he said. 'And me only admiring yer hair!'

I knew straight away that he was a townie, a true blue and a kindred spirit from the city centre. I missed all the people I knew from town, so I immediately crossed the road to talk with him.

We had just moved to a new house again. After Uncle Joseph started living with us, our house in Fortlawn Park seemed much smaller. I had the box room, where we could only fit a single bed. My brothers slept in single beds in the small front bedroom. Mum could barely squeeze a single camp-bed for Joseph alongside her bed in the third bedroom. She had to be careful not to step on her younger brother when she got out of bed.

So she made an application to the Corporation to rent a larger four-bedroomed property. She spotted new social housing being built in Whitestown Drive in Mulhuddart, about a mile away. Mum repeatedly called into the housing office, enquiring about the houses. Finally, Dublin Corporation offered her one there.

'I've just got the keys!' she said as she arrived in the door one late afternoon in June. She was triumphant but nervous. It was too late in the day to move, but she was afraid someone might try to take her house in the meantime. She gathered up my brothers and a few of their friends and packed them off to babysit the house overnight instead. 'Keep the doors locked, and don't let anyone in until I get there tomorrow,' she warned.

We were only living on Whitestown Drive a few days when this stranger remarked about my afro. He told me his name was Noel Day. He and his family had come from Sheriff Street and moved into a new house on the road too. It turned out that he only lived five doors away.

There was something about Noel I warmed to from the first time I met him. As we parted that day after talking about everyone we knew in common from the city centre, he said,

'Drop in anytime and meet the family. We'll have a cup of tea and a proper chat.'

So, days later, I knocked on his front door. His wife answered, and I said, 'I'm here to see Noel. He invited me down for a cup of tea.'

Can you imagine? Here I was, a sixteen-year-old girl calling to the door and telling the wife that her husband had invited me to visit. They were more innocent times because I didn't think about it, and Noel's wife didn't bat an eyelid either.

'Come in, love,' she said. 'I'm Stella.'

They invited me into their home nearly forty years ago now, and I never really left. Noel and Stella didn't just become friends; they became my family.

From the time I met him, Noel and I talked about everything. For whatever reason, we had a connection, and Noel became my surrogate dad. He was far more of a father to me than my biological one. Despite a tough childhood, Noel was a joyful person. I never laughed as much as when I was with him.

He was a hard-working family man who was employed for years in IBM in Mulhuddart, but much more than that, Noel was the most entertaining person I ever spent time around; an amazing man, a real Dublin character. Everyone's day became brighter once they were in his company. He and Stella raised David, Jeff, Andrew and Laura to all be incredible people.

The whole family are interesting and hard-working, and I

love them all. Stella is an absolute lady, who studies Russian, reads poetry and whose idea of a great time is visiting art galleries around the world. She and her eldest son, David, are intelligent, knowledgeable and particularly passionate about history.

Laura is the sister I never had, and we always say that we're the 'thick' ones in the family, with no interest in art, history or poetry. Her daughter, Lucy, is my godchild, who I love like my own. Lucy and I share a passion for music and go to every concert together.

They are my family. Whenever there is a Day family event; a wedding, a christening or a birthday, I am there. Whenever I have a family event, they are right in the heart of it with me. I remember being at a family christening in the city centre, and Jeff introduced me to someone as his sister. The man glanced from me to Jeff, and he looked dubious. When Jeff saw the man's expression, he quipped, 'Are you saying that my mam went off with the postman?'

Having a natural interest in history anyway, Noel's family began exploring their ancestry on his side. I'm always of the opinion that you're better leaving the past where it is. *I don't like dwelling on the past. You know I think it's better to get on with your own life, Jade.*

But Noel's family think otherwise, and they started conducting research into their background. They discovered that this true-blue Dub had a great-great-grandfather who was Black African. It was mad, but I knew those curls of his had to come from somewhere!

Noel's ancestor, Patrick Joseph Day, came from the old British colony of the Gold Coast, now part of Ghana. In more recent years, the family even managed to find an old sepia photograph of the man. He was dark-skinned, very handsome and distinguished with a big silver moustache. He had a regal bearing, emphasised by his elegant suit, white collar and tie.

But the most remarkable thing was his resemblance to Noel and the twinkle in the eye that they both shared. You can see that spark clearly in that old brown-toned photograph. The same sense of mischief came right down the generations to Noel. It was incredible to see the likeness.

Our world imploded when Noel was diagnosed with throat cancer seven years ago. It was a blow, a real shock, but everyone rallied quickly. For three whole years after the diagnosis, we always said, 'Noel will never fucking die. He'll live forever.' He was larger than life, so it seemed impossible that we could ever lose him.

And then the day arrived when they admitted him to Saint Francis Hospice in Blanchardstown, and I had to face the truth. I was about to lose the only real dad I'd ever known. My life revolved around the hospice after that.

I couldn't wait for work to finish so I could get back to Noel. I used to stay by his bedside until after midnight; then I'd go home, go to work and come back the next day, every day.

Whenever a new nurse came in, Noel would introduce me: 'This is my daughter, Dominique, and my other daughter, Laura, will be in later on.'

He always enjoyed it when I'd joke with Laura and say, 'As long as you know *I'm* the favourite daughter.'

One afternoon, when Noel and I were on our own, he smoothed the sheets with his hand and cleared his throat. 'Dominique,' he said. 'Will you do me a favour when I'm gone?'

I could hardly bear to hear him talk like that, but I listened.

'I've been buying flowers for Stella every Valentine's Day since we met,' he said. 'Will you make sure she still gets those flowers every year?'

A ball of grief lodged in my throat, but I promised him, and I kept that pledge and always will.

The day arrived when Noel's breathing became laboured, and he began to slip away from this life. A monk arrived to perform the last rites. Stella beckoned me to come into the room, but the monk didn't see her indicate to me. As everyone entered the room, he stepped in my way and said, 'Sorry, immediate family only.' That's when Stella said, 'She is our family.' She has no idea how much that meant to me.

I was broken-hearted when Noel passed away on Saturday,

30 September 2017. I had only ever attended one family funeral before that. I read at the mass, as did my daughters because Noel was mad about my two girls. To be included in his funeral felt like such a great honour for all of us.

I never cried as hard as I did that day. It only really hit me then that I would never see Noel's smiling face again. I was told afterwards that a person at the funeral saw me and remarked, 'Who's that one? She's crying all day, and she isn't even family.' Someone else turned around and said, 'She is fucking family. Noel adopted her years ago.'

We were included in every single aspect of Noel's life and death by a family with no genetic relationship to us. The lesson I've learned is that family doesn't have to be blood. Blood makes you a relation, but it's love, loyalty and acceptance that makes you family. Family is about the people in your life who you love and who love you, no matter what. I love my mother and brothers and daughters, and they are my blood family.

The Days are my family too. They always see the good in me; they care about my children and me. They are just the loveliest people, and I feel lucky to have found them. It's through these people, who were once strangers, that I have found the wonderful, extended family I never had.

YOUNG AND SINGLE

When I came to Dublin as a child, my one ambition was to get back to London. I had all these fond and distant memories of the place, and the city always called to me. London was on my mind all the time, especially when I finished school. I left to do a secretarial course, like many girls at the time. *There was never any thought of going on to third-level education, Jade. It wasn't an option because there was no money for a luxury like college. I did well to stay in school until I was seventeen.*

While I was doing secretarial training, I worked in a Montessori in Roselawn and in a local store called Sheepmoor Shop, which everyone referred to locally as 'Domo's shop' when I worked there. I also babysat children all around Blanchardstown at night. I was always working and earning a few bob.

London seemed to be the heart of the music and fashion scene back then, and I longed to return. In the mid-eighties, the economy was on its knees in Ireland, and young people were emigrating in large numbers anyway. A lot of Irish teenagers were moving to London. Dublin city wasn't enough for me, and Blanchardstown certainly wasn't enough for me. As far as I was concerned, London was where my future lay. It was always London for me.

By the time I was eighteen years old, I had worked in several jobs for a year and had saved enough money to leave Dublin. I babysat for a woman who arranged accommodation for me with her sister and brother-in-law in Camden town. I told Mum I was going to London for the weekend, and I just didn't come back. I had no intention of ever coming back, if I'm honest. On my second day in London, I got a job in a local newsagent's, and six months after I arrived there, I moved out of shared accommodation into my own bedsit.

I was in my element in London. I hung out in Carnaby Street, the birthplace of the swinging sixties and a mecca for mods, rockers and goths in the eighties. A wave of British designers like Vivienne Westwood, Mary Quant and John Richmond were on the rise. I also hung out in Camden, which was the heart of the punk rock and Teddy boy scene. I loved fashion, so wherever fashion was, I followed.

I loved the style and watching the ever-changing fashion trends of London. There was a youthful excitement about the place with none of the dark sense of recession and economic doom of Dublin. The place was impossibly vibrant, exciting, stylish and colourful for a teenager who had just escaped what seemed like permanent gloom back in Ireland.

I enjoyed the freedom and the choices in London, and I also loved that I didn't stand out. I blended in with all the multicultural and multicoloured youth there. I was like any other teenager for the first time since I'd left London all those years ago. No one wanted to touch my hair or ask where I was really from. Strangers didn't stare at me or call me a Paki.

After a while, though, I began to realise life wasn't easy in London. The wages were low and the rents were sky-high, even then, so it was hard to make ends meet. London is also a lonely city even if friends surround you. Nobody stops to give you a second look, which has its advantages but also disadvantages. I had no support from family over there, and I also felt guilty because I wasn't any support to Mum either, and she was always pressuring me to come home. After two or three years, I returned to Dublin. It was just temporary, I said. I had no intention of staying. The whole idea was to spend a year or two in Dublin, get some savings together and then move back to London again.

I got a job quickly and realised the pay was much better than in London. I began to recognise other differences too. When I'd first returned to London, I was reacquainted with a life where no one knew or cared about their neighbours. Now that I was back in Dublin, I suddenly realised that it was a much friendlier place. It was only in my twenties that I began really appreciating Dublin compared to London.

I also began to get involved in the emerging rave scene in Dublin in the late eighties. The raves were all about love and music, and for the first time in Ireland, my colour never came into it. Everyone at the raves loved you and accepted you. It didn't matter if you were gay or straight, Black or white, male or female, fat or thin. There were no class barriers, and people came to the raves from all over the country. Every event seemed like a welcome party to the world. Differences were pushed aside, and it was all about the music, dance and love. It was a joyful and exciting time to be young.

People think that everyone who was part of the rave scene was off their heads on drink and drugs. The raves never sold alcohol, and ecstasy wasn't part of the early scene. I don't think ecstasy really took off until the 1990s. I know a lot of people who went to the raves and never took drugs. Later on, a lot of people did drugs, but a lot of people didn't.

The craic would start on the buses into town. We would have to split up into groups of ten or so and wait at different bus stops because the drivers would drive straight past us if we were in large groups. Some would bring stereos and blast dance music on the upper deck of the bus, and everyone would have a laugh before we even arrived in town.

It didn't matter what anyone wore. Fellas would arrive in tracksuits, runners and bucket hats and strip down to their shorts. Girls wore tops, shorts, boiler suits or dungarees and sneakers. The clothes had to be loose and cool to allow you to dance all night. I remember a lot of daft neon-coloured gear. Bandanas and smiley-face T-shirts were popular for both sexes.

Being part of a rave was heady stuff. There could be a thousand people dancing like no one was watching. The venues were filled with dry ice, flashing strobe lighting, lasers and the incessant beat of the music. Everyone was loved-up and carefree. There were no fights, and these weren't pick-up joints. Gender didn't come into it. It was all about losing yourself in the beat and the music.

I just remember the great sense of freedom and community. There was also a feeling of connectedness and togetherness. Everyone was beautiful, and everyone was accepted. As the rave scene took off, the places got bigger, and you had clubs like Fantasia, Asylum, the Olympic and the Mansion House. But I'll never forget the early days of the rave scene in Dublin. It was such a good time to be young, a special time.

But it was different in everyday life, where I was reminded on so many occasions about how I looked. In more recent years, for example, I remember waitressing in a golf club and serving a table of five guys.

'Oh my God!' one of the men exclaimed. 'Your English is so good!' He was so shocked that he clutched his chest like he was having a heart attack.

'Thanks,' I said.

'I'm really blown away by how good your English is,' he continued. 'Where are you from?'

'Sean McDermott Street.'

I love saying that just to see people's reaction. You can't get more Dublin than that. He even said it to me in the end: 'You're more Irish than I am.' It's mad that some people are overwhelmed that I can speak English at all. There is always this insistence that you can't have my skin colour and be Irish at the same time.

For two decades or more now, I've been working with children. I love my job because I've always enjoyed being around kids. It's a rewarding job, and I love doing it, but it's also very demanding. Some people like to switch off by going to the gym or jogging, some prefer a bottle of wine, but my favourite way to switch off is shopping. I love shops. I own so much 'stuff' that anyone coming to my house thinks that fifty people must live there. I like nice things. I didn't have anything for many years, so now that I can afford things I like, I enjoy buying them. I used to go to one particular store all the time. At first, I thought I was imagining it, but finally, I realised that I was being followed around by security anytime I visited the store. I tried to ignore it for a while, thinking it would stop, but it didn't.

One day, I was totally fed up. It was ridiculous. Everywhere I went, I could see this man lurking in the rails behind me. I turned around and approached the security guard tailing me and asked him straight out: 'Why do you always follow me around? I'm just shopping. Can't you see that every time I come here, I always leave with bags?'

'I've been told I have to follow you,' he said. The man was apologetic and embarrassed. He said he was only doing his job and following orders. But the store had no reason to suspect me of anything. I've never shoplifted in my life. The only difference between me and the other women in the shop who weren't being followed was my skin colour. There was no point arguing with the security man. Instead, I sent a solicitor's letter to the store. They replied saying it was all a misunderstanding, and they offered me vouchers for the shop as compensation. I didn't want their vouchers, and I didn't accept them.

'I don't want anything,' I said. 'I just want to be able to shop in a store like any other normal person, without feeling harassed.'

That incident is only one example of times I've found myself followed by security. I only have to walk in the door to fall under suspicion in some stores. I earn a good wage, and I pay for my goods. If I can't afford to buy something, I'll wait until I can.

I've never been in trouble with the law. I've been driving twenty-eight years, and I've never even had a speeding ticket nor received a fine or points on my licence. I obey the law. I hate that there is a cloud of suspicion hanging over me just because my skin may be a few shades darker than the average here. It's insane.

There are more and more people of different racial and ethnic identities in Ireland. It should mean that things are getting easier for people who look a bit different. Yet racist abuse still happens.

I remember leaving my brother's house in a brand new Honda Civic. I've always worked for a living, and I was working two jobs at that time. It was a great feeling to have a new car with its new smell and shiny new exterior. As I was getting into the car, these guys across the road started shouting. 'Look at the Black bastard with her new car! Bet you got that for nothing! The government is very generous when it comes to youse lot, aren't they?' They were yelling all this kind of mad stuff.

So these guys saw me, assumed I was a foreigner and that the government had given me a new car. Like most people, I worked hard to buy my car, but I was abused for it and accused of being some kind of freeloader. *I mean, no one gets anything for free, do they?*

My brothers are private people and asked that their lives not be featured in this book, and I have tried to respect that. However, my brother Jason said he was happy to let me share the following experiences from his life.

He sometimes reminds me of things I'd forgotten or tells me about things that I don't remember at all. He remembers our front door in Sean McDermott Street being kicked in all the time. It's strange, but I have no recollection of that. He says that we wedged a chair against the door every night, and he was always getting locked out because when the Corporation fixed the door they changed the locks. I have no idea if our family was targeted specifically or if it happened to everyone in the flats.

Jason was young, but he vividly remembers walking down O'Connell Street when we first arrived in 1978. He says there weren't a lot of cars on the road, but whatever cars were around stopped so the occupants could gawk at us. He remembers Larry coming to Dublin and everyone's heads turning because his skin was so dark. Jason remembers being so embarrassed by all the attention over his dad's colour that he tried to walk ten feet behind his father and pretend he wasn't with him.

Like me, Jason remembers being left to sit outside on my mum's mother's wall. He says we sat there sometimes for an hour and a half. He has even confronted my mum about that. 'I would never, ever do to my kids what you did to us,' he told her.

School was a war zone for my brothers. I never knew until recently, too, that Jason hated the song 'Brown Girl in the Ring' as much as I did. The boys would surround him and sing it to him. Can you believe that?

Shortly after starting school in Dublin, Jason remembers

one of the boys announcing to the class, 'Look, I'm sitting beside a bar of chocolate.' Jason was used to school in England, where no one paid any attention to his skin colour. He was bewildered and started crying because of all the jeering over the 'chocolate' comment. When the teacher came in, he hit Jason so hard that he broke his ruler over his hands – all because he was crying in his classroom. Jason was seven years old.

Both my brothers ended up leaving school when they were only aged twelve and in their first year of secondary school. They could handle bullying from some students, but they couldn't cope with the brutal treatment they received from teaching staff and school authorities. The abuse they got was constant, and I think it must have been a race thing. They were good, well-behaved kids, yet first one and then the other was picked on by the school authorities. It was so vicious how they were driven from the school. Despite being deprived of an education, they are now businessmen who have done very well in life, but their success is mostly due to our mother's unwavering support. When I think back, we were let down badly by teachers and those adults whose job was to educate and protect us. They did the very opposite at times.

When he was a young teenager and in secondary school in Blanchardstown, I decided to bring my brother James to the barbershop to have his afro shaved off. I wanted him to look more like the rest of the boys and not attract the attention of the bullies. I felt bad because my brother cried all the way home on the bus, devastated at losing his afro.

But Jason told me recently that, years later, James did the same thing to him. I never knew a thing about it, but when Jason was around ten or twelve years old, James brought him to the barbershop for a 'trim'. He secretly instructed the barber to drive his shaver down the middle of Jason's head so that he would have to crop off the lot. Jason said he came out with so little hair that he was freezing.

'No one's going to bother you now,' his older brother told him.

Jason even says his brother still goes to the same barber after all these years.

We recalled another time when we were young, and this girl said to me, 'Why didn't you tell us you were adopted?'

'Because I'm not,' I said.

'Being adopted is nothing to be ashamed of,' she insisted. 'There's nothing to be embarrassed about.'

'I know, but I'm not adopted.'

'I know you are.'

'But I'm not – where are you getting this from?'

'Jason told my brother youse are all adopted.'

I was bewildered by why Jason would say that. I said to him that night, 'Why are you going around telling people we're adopted?'

'It's easier than explaining,' he replied.

When I thought about it, I had to admit he had a point.

His colour still affected him, even as a working man. A few years ago, Jason pulled up to start some construction work on a premises. A woman was walking past, and she stopped and said accusingly, 'What are you doing here?' Jason just ignored her and went in and continued working. An hour or so later, two men arrived and said they were from immigration.

'Where are you from?' one of them asked.

'Why? What's the matter?' my brother replied.

'Well, that answers that.' The immigration guy laughed, knowing straight away from his accent that he was from Dublin. He said they had a call from a concerned citizen saying an illegal immigrant was working on the premises.

Life is much better for people of colour today, but racial abuse still happens. Jason says he was in a shop with his little boy when another child came in and said, 'Hi Jayden.' Jason was surprised when his son completely ignored the boy.

'That was very rude of you not to answer that little boy,' Jason said outside. 'I didn't bring you up to be rude to people.'

Jason discovered from another source days later that boy had called Jayden a 'n***er' at school, and that's why he wouldn't reply to him. Kids don't always tell you what's going on.

Jason went through so much growing up that he decided his children should be taught how to defend themselves.

He and his wife, Debbie, sent their four kids to kick-boxing training due to his childhood experiences. They thought it would give the kids greater confidence and courage in the face of the inevitable bullying they would encounter. I mean, that's crazy when you think about it, isn't it?

I think the simple truth is that most people of colour would just like to get through life without being reminded of their colour all the time. I know I would.

MY GIRLS

I didn't let many people know that I was expecting my first child. I was in my early twenties, and I figured that it wasn't anyone else's business but my own. I was able to keep my pregnancy to myself until very late because my bump was tiny. I just remember being so happy when I discovered I was expecting Jade. I worked almost right up until my due date and looked forward to becoming a mum.

I was already well in labour when I presented at the Rotunda Hospital. The midwife asked me if a junior doctor from South Africa could perform the delivery. He was tall, fair-haired and jittery, as this was his first baby.

Jade was born at 7.40 p.m. on 3 October 1988, within hours of me arriving at the Rotunda. She was two weeks late and 6 lbs 2 ounces in weight. Her name reflects my love of everything green. The couches, carpets and walls in my place are green, and jade stone is linked with luck, health, wealth and love.

The doctor who delivered Jade was obsessed with her from the minute she was born, and I couldn't blame him. She was a beautiful baby, with big dark eyes, long lashes and a full head of hair. Everyone was mesmerised by her. Shortly after her birth, the doctor approached me again.

'Can I dress her for you?' he asked.

I thought it was a bit odd, but I gave him the bag of new baby clothes I'd brought to the hospital. When he came back with Jade, he looked very proud of himself. She was wearing a neon lemon Babygro and a peach knitted cardigan. It was my baby's first ever outfit, and the mix of colours looked dreadful.

I remember whispering to one of the other mums in horror, 'I have so many lovely clothes for her, but look what he did!'

I couldn't hurt his feelings by changing her straight away, but I couldn't wait until he finished his shift to get that outfit off her.

That doctor kept calling to see her several times a day. *I started raising my eyes to heaven when I saw him coming. I used to say that he was stalking you, Jade, because he used any excuse to visit you.* I know he delivered her, but he was as proud of her as if she was his own. There was another nurse who was nearly as bad. He and that nurse used to carry her around the wards and show her to everybody.

'Oh my God, she's so beautiful,' the nurse kept saying.

'Every baby is beautiful,' I said.

'Oh no,' said the nurse, shaking her head sadly. 'I've seen babies that only a mother could love.'

I couldn't believe a nurse would say that.

Jade's arrival put an end to any lingering thoughts of returning to London. It's one thing going to a big city when you're young and single, but it's different when you have a child. I had to work for a living, and there was no way I'd let a stranger mind my child in England. I had my mum in Dublin, who was more than willing to take Jade, and from day one, she was brilliant with the baby. She just adored her, and Jade adored her grandmother. I was able to go back to work when Jade was two weeks old and know she was well cared for.

Jade had a local fan club from the time she was born. Several of my brothers' friends used to call all the time to see her. They kept offering to take Jade to the park in her pram. I was astonished by how caring they were and how interested they were in her as a baby. It was fantastic. The lads used to give Mum or me a break for an hour or more some days. I knew I could call any of them to mind her and they would come running, even at short notice. The guys would even fight over who'd bring her to the park.

'Aren't they so good to want to take her out all the time?' I used to say to my mum. 'You'd never think that boys would be so thoughtful.'

It was years later before I learned what had really gone on – that they had wheeled her around the park to get the attention of girls. They used to make up these terrible stories saying that their girlfriend had died or that she had walked out on them and left them with the baby. Jade was a gorgeous baby, and the girls used to flock around them when they had her. Jade was just a handy prop for them to meet girls. They used her as their 'babe magnet'.

She was such an easy baby. I had to wake her to feed her because otherwise she would have slept through the night. I adored her. I loved to spend my money on lovely dresses for her and to plait her big hair and bead it. She started dancing as soon as she walked at ten months old. She loved music, and *Top of the Pops* was her favourite programme as it had been mine years earlier. She always made me laugh when she toddled over to the telly and kissed it and bopped in her nappy when *Top of the Pops* was on. I don't know how she isn't wearing glasses now because she'd have her nose pressed to the TV whenever music was on. I bought her toy guitars, keyboards and microphones, and she loved performing with them and singing all the wrong words. She still sings all the wrong words to this day.

When I lived in London, I enjoyed performing in the shows we staged in the Girl Guides. As a teenager in Dublin, I joined drama classes after school. I used to catch the bus from Blanchardstown into the city centre and take the train to Ballsbridge to study with Miss Meredith in the Oscar Theatre School. I looked forward to those classes so much that I worked after school every day to pay for them. Performance was something that appealed to me, so I thought Jade might like it too.

She hadn't even started school when I brought her to Irish dancing. She went twice, but she didn't take to it. I brought her to the National Performing Arts School in the city centre instead, and that was a love affair from the start. As soon as she wore her dance shoes or had a microphone in her hand, she was in her element. Straightaway, she was a little star. She loved singing and dancing and adored being in that school.

Many high-profile parents had children in the school then. Taoiseach Bertie Ahern's girls and broadcaster Gerry Ryan's kids attended the classes. Keavy and Edele Lynch, twin sisters of Boyzone's Shane Lynch, were in Jade's classes before they went on to become the stars of the pop group, B*Witched. But it didn't matter who you were or how talented you were, every child was encouraged. There was a great atmosphere in the place, and creativity and fun were prioritised.

Jade was sent to auditions when she was suitable for parts, and she appeared in various shows and advertisements. Assets Model Agency approached me and asked to sign her to their books, so she began modelling for stores like Marks & Spencer. Jade was never happier than when she was modelling clothes. If I let her, she would have changed her clothes five or six times a day. She regularly appeared on the children's programme *Disney Club* on RTÉ2. She even landed a big TV advert to be shot in America one time, but I couldn't leave her little sister or take the time off from work to do it.

Jade was seven years old when her little sister, Pariss, arrived on 20 July 1995. She was born at 1.40 p.m., less than twenty minutes after I arrived at the hospital, weighing 6 lbs 12 oz. She was a beautiful newborn, a much longer or taller baby than Jade, with a full head of black hair.

Whether I had a boy or a girl that day, the baby was going to be called Pariss. I had a passion for the French capital, even though I had never been there at that stage. The city seemed so cosmopolitan and glamorous; something about the place drew me. But friends and family were having heart attacks at the prospect of calling the baby Pariss.

'Pariss? Oh God, really?' was the response.

No one had heard of the name then. It was a few years later that Michael Jackson named his child Paris and Paris Hilton arrived on the scene. Actor Pierce Brosnan named his son Paris less than a decade later. People didn't get it as a name.

'Well, thank God she's a girl rather than a boy,' they said after Pariss was born. 'You can get away with that name for a girl.'

Amazingly, Jade showed no jealousy at all when the new baby arrived. She doted on her little sister from the start. They were completely different children – I couldn't believe how much. Pariss started to walk at nine months, and once she started walking, she broke everything in sight. She would just pick things up and smash them off the ground and laugh, delighted with herself.

Their interests were completely different. Jade was into music and dancing from the beginning, while Pariss was obsessed with animals from the time she was tiny. While Jade worshipped *Top of the Pops*, Pariss grew up glued to National Geographic Channel. It was her favourite television station. She loved reading books from the time she was a tot too.

If I bought you a book, you'd cry, Jade. I remember one time I gave you a book along with your Easter egg, and you said, 'You think you're smart, don't you?' You thought I'd given you a book as a joke or to annoy you!

I bought Pariss an animal book from Smyths toy store every week, and she'd pore over it, reading it from cover to cover for days. Every time someone came through the door, she'd latch onto them and bring out her latest book and tell them everything about the animal. She was such an intelligent child. She was like a tiny professor, and every visitor would be forced to sit there and hear everything they never wanted to know about the screaming hairy armadillo or the duck-billed platypus. Or she'd frighten the life out of them, telling them about killer jellyfish or bird-eating spiders.

Her teacher sent a letter home to me when she started in first class. He said he had a problem with Pariss because she wanted to take out adult books in the library rather than choosing books from the children's section. I told him that I didn't see it as a problem. I wasn't going to stop her from reading what she was able to read.

Like every mum, I wanted the best for my children, and I wanted them to have opportunities that I didn't have. Most of all, I wanted them engaged in both learning and creative pursuits. I wanted them to explore their interests. Unfortunately, I soon discovered that after-school activities and hobbies could add up to a lot of money. Jade spent Saturdays and Sundays and after school in the National Performing Arts School. She joined every class, from street dance, funk, modern dance and drama to singing lessons and musical theatre. It cost a small fortune each year to attend all those classes.

Performing, singing, dancing and acting was and remains Jade's world. She loved it. She never expressed a desire to do anything else. The performing arts world is hard and not an easy career to succeed in, but I would never stand in my children's way. I'm happy that she found her passion, so I didn't mind when she said she would follow that dream after school. If she wanted to be a bus driver or work on a supermarket check-out, I would have supported her too.

The great love Pariss had for animals never faded. She loved horses, so she became interested in riding every weekend. She became a fantastic horse-rider and began taking part in show jumping. I bought her two horses during those years when she was growing up, and this meant paying monthly livery costs in stables in Ashbourne and later in Dunboyne.

I took on several jobs to pay for it all. I had a full-time job working with children every day and an evening job as an office cleaner. At nights and weekends, I also did waitressing. I worked many hours when the kids were small, and my mum did a lot of the childminding. It took a lot of juggling and a lot of work to ensure the girls got every chance they deserved. Sometimes things were hectic, but that was the cost of giving the girls the childhood and the opportunities I didn't have. That was important to me.

Each year, I also made sure to save enough money for us all to have a holiday in the sun together. Like my mum brought me to Ireland for holidays as a kid, I wanted my children to experience going abroad too. I never wanted them to feel they were losing out on anything because they only had one parent to provide for them. It was important to me that we had lots of fun together when they were growing up. I wanted them to have lots of happy childhood memories, and going on family holidays to Spain or wherever in the summer was a part of that.

Before Jade went to secondary school, I took her out of the modelling agency. I didn't want to give anyone any reason to pick on her. Maybe I had a hunch about what was going to happen, but there were still instances when she got bullied.

Like all teenagers, she started drinking too. Pariss did the same years later. I never drank, nor did her grandmother, and I certainly didn't allow underage drinking. One night Jade arrived in, and I instantly knew what she'd been up to.

'You've been drinking.'

'No, I haven't.'

'You have.'

'I haven't,' she insisted, and then she promptly passed out in the hall right in front of me. Jade was grounded, and so was Pariss in her time. Then they both went out and did it all over again.

Then there was the time that the principal rang me to say that Jade hadn't been in school. It was a huge shock to me because I was dropping her off at the school most days. The first person I rang was my mum. I knew if Jade was hiding out anywhere, it was in her place. The two of them were incredibly close, and they still are. She was the first grandchild. 'Jade's my treasure,' she always says.

'Why didn't you tell me Jade's been mitching from school and staying with you?'

Mum denied it. 'I don't know what you're talking about. She's not here.'

I'd swear if Jade robbed a bank, my mum would cover for her.

'If she's not there with you, I have to get the guards involved. So, you'd better admit she's there, or I'm putting down the phone and calling the police.'

The threat of the guards was the only reason she admitted Jade was with her instead of being in school.

I want my children to have every opportunity in life. To do that, I knew they needed to go to school and to college, but Mum didn't think like that.

'If she doesn't want to go to school, she has her reasons,' she would say.

Mum spoilt them. I made nutritious lunches for my kids for school. My mum would give them whatever they wanted. I'd never let children have coffee. She gave it to them instead.

I was the one who was always saying 'No, they can't do this' or 'They can't have that!'

And my mum would say, 'Ah, sure, let them. They're only young once.'

She's loving and caring, but she panders to them, and that's not the way I wanted my children to be brought up. I had rules. There's nothing worse than children who are brought up with no manners or feel entitled because they get everything they want. Mum had no boundaries when it came to kids. She couldn't say no to my girls or anyone else.

Pariss was the least likely of the two girls to be bullied growing up. She can be emotional and soft, but she has this look that can stop anyone in their tracks. In that way, Pariss is a lot like me. No one messes her around. She's well able to stand up to anyone and say 'get out my face'. One night, I remember four of us – myself, Pariss, Jade and a friend of Jade's – in the sitting room watching telly. We were living in Charnwood in Clonsilla at the time. Over the sound of the TV, we heard a disturbance outside. We turned down the sound, and we could hear a gang chanting 'Pakis out! Pakis out!' on the street. I think I just raised my eyes to heaven because being called a 'Paki' is just tiresome at this stage.

Pariss looked out, and she recognised the culprits as a few guys her age from the estate. We ignored them until there was a loud bang, and a jagged crack appeared across our sitting-room window. They had thrown a rock at the house. This time, we didn't hesitate. We all scrambled to our feet and ran out in every direction. We were all angry. I was livid over the cracked window. Jade was furious over them trying to bully her little sister. Jade's friend was mad that we had to experience that kind of bullshit. And Pariss … it doesn't take much for Pariss to get mad. We caught the lads, and let's just say they never came around to call Pariss a Paki again.

Later that evening, our next-door neighbour came to the door looking very apologetic. 'I heard all those lads shouting,' she said. 'And I said to Paddy, "There's a gang of lads outside next door. Get out there and help Dominique!" I'm sorry, Dominique, but Paddy wouldn't budge. He said, "I'm not putting a foot out there. Dominique is well able to look after herself!"'

We all laughed at that because he's right. I've learned to look after myself because I had to. Being a different colour than most has made me harder than I should be. No child should be left sitting on a wall or made to feel like an outsider because of the colour of their skin. It has been easier for Jade and Pariss and, hopefully, easier again for the coming generation. So, Paddy was right. I am well able to look after myself. I had to. We've had a fair bit of hassle over the years, and I don't like to talk about it, but I absolutely refuse to tolerate it.

Jade

DIRTY

One day I was a typical kid, and the next day I wasn't. That's how quickly a momentous thing can happen and change your life, isn't it?

For Nanny, it was the day two guards arrived at the door to break the news about her father's illness. For Ma, it was coming to Ireland. Ma was an ordinary girl until she moved to Dublin, and then she felt she was apart, different from everyone else. It was while writing Nanny and Ma's stories that I recalled the watershed moment in my life.

It happened when I was ten years old, and I argued with a boy, a row that was only significant because it was the first time I realised there was something different about me. Until that day, I lived in a world where I thought I was the same as everyone else. I went to school, and I sang, and I danced, and I played with lots of other kids and was like any other girl.

After that fight, I saw someone entirely different when I looked in the mirror. I became conscious of something I had been wholly unconscious about for the first ten years of my life. That silly little childhood spat also led to developing an obsessive-compulsive behaviour that lasted for years.

It all happened in McDonough's Caravan Park in Bettystown in County Meath. Bettystown, with its miles of long sandy beaches, was always a traditional summer-holiday destination for Dubliners. My nanny's father had family, a sister or someone, in Mornington, about two miles up the coast at the mouth of the River Boyne. Nanny had vague but fond childhood memories of the area. She can't remember much about it now, but she always associated the area with her father, sunshine and beaches. So, she saved up enough to buy a small second-hand mobile home in McDonough's park in the mid-nineties and gave us a treasure chest of brilliant childhood memories to cherish too.

As soon as she bought the mobile home, we started spending all our summers there. Mam always brought us on foreign holidays too, but we spent the months of the school summer holidays in Bettystown. Pariss was just a toddler at the time, so I played with loads of other kids my age in the park. I loved our summer holidays in Bettystown and couldn't wait to get to the mobile home every year.

For our entire school summer holidays, we lived in the mobile. There was Pariss, my cousin Donna, my great-uncle Joseph and me. Donna is my uncle Jason's daughter, so she is mixed-race like me, but has a paler complexion. With her blonde hair and blue eyes, she looks completely different to me. The adults used to come and go, but Nanny was the one constant. We loved our nanny, and we were always clambering over her. She had this fine, long silky hair, and we loved brushing it. It also gave us an excuse to poke the two holes in her head, a permanent reminder of her lobotomy. We were fascinated by those two holes in her scalp. They were near the front of her head, on both sides of her skull, and we'd see how much of our fingers would disappear when we pushed them in. When I think back, she had the patience of Job with us.

Nanny stayed with us all the time, except on Fridays when she had to take the bus back to Dublin to collect her pension. Nanny, always suspicious of the bank and the post office, had to collect it every Friday for fear that it would be gone if she delayed. To this day, she still feels her pension is only safe when she has it in her own handbag.

Our neighbours on the caravan site came from all across Dublin's northside, stretching from Sheriff Street in the city centre to the suburban areas of Coolock, Donaghmede, Kilbarrack, Blanchardstown and Cabra. The same families came to McDonough's every summer, so we knew everyone, and everyone knew us. It was a great little community.

At the entrance to McDonough's site, I remember a thatched pub on the left and another thatched house on the right-hand side with a little sausage dog. All the kids loved to play with that dog. The site owners positioned all the big, fancy mobile homes at the front of the site where the office was located. The office had a small hatch from which the owners sold bread, milk and basic groceries. They also sold chips in flimsy white plastic containers, and we coated our chips in orange-hued tomato sauce from the squeezy red bottles sitting by the hatch.

The office also became the site of a kids' disco when I was about nine years old. It was the best of fun as we leapt about in our tracksuits to music from the Spice Girls, Scooter and TLC. Then 'Spice up Your Life' was interrupted by one eleven-year-old young one accusing another of looking at her fella. Within minutes, everyone took sides, murder broke out, and the first disco night was brought to a premature end amid chaos. We were given a final warning the next week, but the second disco ended even sooner. Mr McDonough caught us soaking loo rolls in the toilet and flinging globs of soggy paper to his ceiling, where they hung like ugly polka dots.

'Get out, youse little shits! Get out!' he roared, and that was the last of McDonough's disco nights.

Our mobile was located at the back of the site, sage green in colour with a cream and brown stripe. It was tiny, a hybrid of a caravan and a mobile home. The skip for the rubbish was on one side of us, and the playground was on the other. 'Playground' is a bit of a fancy title for essentially two rusting swings and a slide. Donna and I always stood on the swings and called for someone to give us a starting push. Then we'd use our body weight to accelerate and build up the momentum until we couldn't get any faster or higher. As it came to the point where it seemed we'd turn a full revolution on the swing, we'd leap off mid-air, shrieking in terror and delight. We could have killed ourselves, but when you're ten, having a laugh outweighs the risks of breaking your neck.

Our playground had a sandpit as well. The sand was lying there for years, so was more of an unofficial litter box for the local cats than a sandpit. That was probably why Ma warned us that if we got sand in our hair the grains would turn into nits. Oh my God, there was nothing on the planet scarier for Donna and me than the prospect of creepy crawlies on our heads. The rest of the kids must have been gullible too because they all believed my ma's nits story. Everyone stayed well away from the sandpit.

McDonough's Caravan Park was five minutes from the beach and 'the village', which consisted of a chipper, an amusement arcade, a Chinese restaurant and Pat's shop. The shop sold a bit of everything. We could buy our bread, milk and sausages at the counter, and I could post a letter for Nanny in the post office at the back of the shop.

All the kids loved the Chinese for their 'salad burgers'. They assembled the gourmet burgers with a rubber bun, a lettuce leaf, a sliver of onion and a blob of mayonnaise on an overdone patty of mince. Yet they were considered the best burgers on the planet. Maybe the secret ingredient was the sunshine or the sea air because, honest to God, we still talk about the salad burgers in Bettystown.

The amusement 'arcade' was just a shack with a few slot machines. But 'the slots', as we called the place, was the meeting point in the village. 'Are youse coming to the slots?' the kids would say. 'See youse outside the slots tonight.' We always got a buzz out of banging the machines or shoving another kid into them to make the money fall out. We'd only have seconds to gather up the coins from the chute before the owner came bellowing. Jesus, there was nothing more exhilarating than getting chased out of the slots with fistfuls of stolen change. We were always getting barred.

Our nanny never darkened the door of the slots. 'I'm not into that gambling,' she'd say, like it was Caesar's Palace instead of a few one-armed bandits in a shed. Unfortunately, Ma liked the slots, so we'd be sweating with nerves when she arrived to Bettystown. As soon as she'd say, 'Let's go down to the slots,' we'd run in every direction. We knew if the owner saw us, he'd tell Ma we'd been robbing money out of the machines, and Ma would kill us. She'd bloody murder us for any kind of messing like that.

It's funny, we were living minutes from the beach, yet I don't remember us ever playing in the water. Isn't that weird? It's only recently that I started sea swimming, and the feeling of freedom and relaxation it gives me is amazing. Yet, I don't remember any of us being in the sea as kids.

Sometimes, we'd catch the bus from Bettystown to Drogheda. It was a coach rather than a double-decker bus, and Donna and I'd be raging if someone else nabbed the seats behind the bus driver. It seemed that the journey along the winding country lanes took forever, but it was probably only half an hour. As soon as we got into Drogheda, we'd make a beeline for Saint Peter's church to see Oliver Plunkett's head. The scary head in its glass case was the must-see of every trip to Drogheda. Kids are always fascinated by the ghoulish, aren't they? We'd spend ages gawping at this four-hundred-year-old relic, marvelling over his white teeth and brown leather face. We'd always light a candle too, but Oliver Plunkett's mummified head was the big attraction.

Usually, Nanny would have given us a tenner spending money for our trip to Drogheda, so we'd head for the shop in the town that sold knick-knacks and ornaments. We always had to buy Nanny something as our way of saying thank you. When I look back now, the ornaments were hideous plastic things, but we always wanted to bring something back for Nanny. We adored her.

When we discovered that Nanny loved the green marzipan cakes they sold in the cake shop in Drogheda, we'd go there instead. We couldn't afford the full cake, so they would slice it in two, and we would present half a green marzipan to Nanny.

One day, I spotted a glass tea-set in the ornament shop. It had two glass cups, saucers, plates and maybe a sugar bowl, and the glass had this hideous pinkish hue. I thought it was deadly, the perfect present for my nanny. I saved hard to buy it, and I was so proud of giving her a whole tea-set in a box. Unfortunately, I believed this gift was so amazing that Nanny got it with lots of strings attached. Every time we had words, any bit of a row at all, I'd glower at her and demand the set back. Nanny would have to take it down off the shelf and give it back to me. I'd stuff the set among my clothes and things and guard it jealously. When Nanny and I were friends again, I'd feel bad and return the set to her. She'd have to put the set all back on display again, and this routine went on for years.

'Oh, Jade, you used to break my heart with that pink tea-set,' she says, but she still has it.

My ma was incredibly strict about the time I had to be home. She was a sergeant-major about curfews, and I never dared stay out a minute late. Even when I was eighteen, she would have had me in at 10 p.m. if she had her way. But in Bettystown, we felt like we were running wild because Nanny never called us in until dark. In reality, there was nothing wild about it. All the kids played together, and all the parents sat out and watched us. God, we had the best of times in Bettystown.

Nanny and Ma never drank in their lives, but Uncle Joseph was allowed one can of Murphy's Irish Stout on special occasions like Christmas and his birthday. I don't know how this tradition started – it must have been something that came from the time he lived with his mother. One day, my nanny had to go out, and she told us we weren't to move from the mobile home.

'You're all to stay and look after Joseph,' she said. 'Don't take your eye off him for a minute!'

It was just me and my cousin Donna, and one of us came up with the idea of giving Joseph a beer. We spotted the cans of Murphy's stout on a high shelf in the caravan. I don't know why they were there at all. Anyway, we gave Joseph a can, and he was delighted. So we decided to give him another one, and Joseph was even happier. He was smiling from ear to ear and clapping and having a great time. He never got two beers in his life. We started acting the maggot then and gave him a third can of beer. It was all very funny until Joseph's eyes started rolling, his head began bobbing, and he slid down in his seat.

'Jesus, he's locked!' I said.

We were kids. We didn't know what to do.

'Oh my God, what if he never comes back to normal again?' Donna asked, petrified. 'What if we've done this to him permanently?'

'Oh, Sacred Heart of Jesus,' I said. 'Nanny is going to kill us.'

We were panicked and shouting.

'Is everything all right?' Mrs Connolly hollered from mobile behind us. She was keeping an eye on us with Nanny gone. We could see her standing on the steps of her mobile, squinting as she tried to look inside ours. If she came over, we were dead.

'Yes, we're only messin',' Mrs Connolly!' Donna called, and we stuffed our fists in our mouths and hoped to God that she wouldn't come over and look in.

Between the two of us, we managed to get Joseph into bed. We stuffed the empty cans of Murphy's down the bottom of the skip, and when Nanny came home, we told her that Joseph got tired and wanted to go to bed. I was petrified that when he woke he would still be drunk. I thought we might have broken him or poisoned him or something by giving him too many cans.

We were mad about our Uncle Joseph. Everyone loved him. Down syndrome has many levels of severity, and his was quite severe as he was non-verbal. Things might have been different if he'd had the kind of opportunities kids with Down syndrome have now, but there was nothing back then. He let Nanny know when he wanted to use the toilet, but he could feed himself if we mashed his food. He was strong and heavy, but he was the gentlest of souls and adored small children and babies. He brought our family so much joy and love. He was our lucky charm and our special child, and we all believe he was a gift to our family.

Our neighbours in Whitestown were good to him too. People would bring him newspapers because he enjoyed tearing them. Ripping up newspapers was great gas to him.

The neighbours would collect the ripped papers for their fires when he was finished. Ma's best friend, Laura, would bring him presents like a toy gun for his birthday or Christmas, and he'd run around pretending to shoot everyone even though he was in his fifties. Joseph loved cowboy movies, and he would sit there with his hands clasped, rocking in his seat and watching them for hours and hours. He was so happy watching a cowboy movie.

Joseph brought so much fun and happiness to our house. He loved being in the mobile home in Bettystown when he'd have all of us sleeping in the one place. He was never happier than when he had all his family around him. I dread to think of the life Joseph would have had if my nanny hadn't taken him out of Portrane. He lived with us for more than twenty years, and I was fourteen years old when he died on 15 November 2002. He was in his sixties, which was considered a great age for someone with Down Syndrome then. He was loved by us all. Nanny was heartbroken, and she never fully recovered from his passing.

I don't think Joseph was around the day I had the fight with the boy. I remember so much detail about the incident, but, strangely, I can't remember for sure who was there. As a kid, I was a tomboy and lived in tracksuits. That day, I know I was wearing a navy Adidas tracksuit with three lime-green stripes down the side of the top and pants, and I had a pair of Nike runners with a blue tick. My runners were immaculate.

I always carried a baby wipe in case I might get a mark on them. (Nanny had packets of wipes everywhere for cleaning up Joseph.) The kids used to jeer me, but I still carry wipes in my handbag for my shoes. Clean shoes are one of my *things*.

The lad I fought with had been one of my first ever 'boyfriends'. When I say boyfriend, I use the term lightly because we were only ten or eleven years old when we went out. He was a friend of a friend and about a year older than me, so he was twelve that summer. He was also slightly taller than me, with carefully gelled brown hair and a freckled face. He was a good-looking chap who grew even more handsome as he grew older. Let's call him Eoin because I don't want to blame him or embarrass him, but he played an integral part in my early story.

Eoin was sitting outside our mobile home. We had no wooden decking around our mobile in those days. We just had a set of white plastic garden furniture on the grass outside. My nanny, God love her, had broken her back working to buy the full set.

I remember glancing over at Eoin, and I realised he had a lighter in his hands and was burning the side of one of Nanny's plastic chairs. I went ballistic. I ran over and thumped him in the arm. 'Get your lighter away from that, yeh eejit! Me nanny is after paying good money for that chair!'

Eoin jumped up, and his face was flushed red from either rage or embarrassment. I'm not sure.

'Don't you touch me, yeh dirty Paki!' he said.

They were his words.

'Who are you calling a dirty Paki?' I replied, even though I didn't even know what the word meant. 'Yer a dirty eejit! You and your stupid lighter!'

Eoin yanked up his sleeve and jabbed his forefinger into a milky-white arm. 'Whose skin looks dirtier then, yours or mine?' he said. 'Whose? Yours does!'

He stomped off down the mobile site, walking backwards most of the way, shouting, 'Yeh dirty yoke, yeh!'

I tried to pretend that I didn't care, but the row shook me. I remembered Eoin pointing at his white arm, and I looked at mine, and I thought, *My arm does look dirty compared to his.*

I remember going into the mobile home and getting into the tiny shower. I felt upset. Once I was out of sight of everyone, I started sobbing. I was in an awful state. I can remember standing in the shower, scrubbing and scrubbing and lifting my arm to re-examine it and then scrubbing it again until my skin was burning red.

It was the first time that I'd ever really noticed the colour of my skin. *Is this dirt,* I wondered, *or is it the colour of my skin? Or is the colour of my skin dirty?* I'd never been self-conscious about how I looked before. He said I looked dirty, but I didn't want to look dirty. *Do I look dirty?*

I kept scrubbing myself, thinking my skin would get

lighter and I might start to look cleaner. I was trying to wash my colour off me; trying to wash myself white. I remember coming out of the shower and sobbing to my nanny. 'I just want to be like everybody else!'

I didn't want anyone looking at me and seeing me as any different from all the other kids.

I always had a thing for cleaning anyway. I'm like my mother, maybe worse. I was a fusspot, and dirt was a massive phobia for me. I mean, how many kids do you know who carry around baby wipes for their shoes? I'd have a conniption if a bit of yoghurt or ice cream got on my clothes, so I used to change outfits all the time. My poor nanny had to lug bags of washing to the launderette lady on the caravan site all the time. But washing became a bigger obsession for me after that incident.

Long after I realised that cleaning was never going to change my colour, I was still washing myself. It triggered something already in my head because I started showering three or four times a day. Nanny and Ma complained all the time about me 'living' in the shower. This continued for years, and the truth is it still continues today.

That incident with Eoin sticks out in my mind so well. I remember it in so much detail that I'm sure I'll hold that memory in my head until the day I die. I don't bear any grudge or resentment against him. We were kids, and kids say things, cruel things, and say things they overhear and don't necessarily understand. The next day we were out playing together again like nothing ever happened.

I still know Eoin, and I bumped into him a couple of times this year. We'd never pass each other without saying 'hello, how are you?' He'll always ask, 'How's your nanny?' I'm sure he doesn't remember a thing about that incident all those years ago. If I turned around now and told him that story, I think he'd be genuinely upset. He has no clue that this was a pivotal point for me when I was growing up.

As I said, we were kids. I had plenty of fights before that evening and plenty more afterwards. That one is only significant because it was the first time I realised I was different from the other kids.

I stared in the mirror in the mobile home that night and saw something I'd never seen before. I saw the dusky skin under my shock of wiry hair, and I saw the dark brown eyes like it was for the first time. My colour had been hiding in plain sight all along.

LEAVING

My nanny went to London as a young woman; so did my ma. It's only while writing this book, I've realised how history has a habit of repeating itself.

When we were twenty years old, my best friend Fiona and I decided we were going to London, and we were never coming back. Ever. So it was frustrating, to say the least, when the woman at the airport check-in desk regarded all our worldly possessions with implacable hostility.

'Your cases are not getting on this plane,' she said. She was emphatic about it.

We looked at our matching carry-on luggage: two huge rectangular cases, big enough to hold a couple of sumo wrestlers. They weighed like they did too. The cases were so vast that looked more like cows than suitcases. So, they were known as 'the cows'.

That day, I was moving to London with the hope of one day appearing in the West End. My lifelong dream was to be in musical theatre. My brain was always miles away from my books, and by fifth and sixth year in secondary, I was forever on the mitch. I was never academic. Singing, dancing and acting were the only things that interested me from the age of four. I lived for my classes in the National Performing Arts School every weekend.

The movie *Fame* was one of my favourite films, and I watched it over and over. The National Performing Arts School was like a real-life movie set to me. Oh God, it was brilliant! When we moved to The Factory in Barrow Street, we'd see the members of U2 arriving to rehearse in the room next door or actor Colin Farrell strolling around between his rehearsals. There was such a buzz around the school. All walks of life hung out there, and the whole atmosphere was positive, encouraging and creative. Once I walked in the door of the place, I didn't want to leave.

At first, going to secondary school was great too. I was one of the only mixed-race girls in the school, and I'd been to only all-girls schools in primary. This was my first time in a mixed-sex or co-ed school, so it was a new adventure for me. I made lots of friends and was welcomed into a group of new girlfriends. But then there was a falling out, and God, girls can be vicious. I felt the full power of their exclusion tactics, nasty comments and back-stabbing. One day, I had lots of friends, and the next day, I had none. Loads of people ostracised me. Everyone knew I was the girl who no one should talk to for fear all the 'cool' girls might turn on them also.

That's around the time I started trying to change my hair. Like all kids that age, I wanted to blend in, disappear into the background and be like everyone else. My hair was long black spiral waves, and when I was growing up, those curls extended right down the length of my back to my bum. I look back on photographs now, and I realise my natural hair was gorgeous. But understanding your place in the world is hard when you have no role models. My ma always told me I was beautiful, but there wasn't anyone who looked like me in magazines or on TV in Ireland then.

I wanted to look like everyone else, to fit in, so I started using chemical straighteners to realise my dreams of having long, silky hair. Of course, the chemicals didn't work. My hair looked a disaster. I was at that age when kids experiment too, so I dyed it red and cut it short and shaved the sides. I couldn't leave it alone. I was never happy with my hair. I put so many chemicals on my head that my hair started breaking off, and it never recovered. I would do anything to revive the natural curls I was born with. I've gone to specialists and spent thousands of euros over the last decade trying to reverse the damage I did, but nothing has worked. My hair is thin and brittle, and all its original vibrancy and curls are gone. It has been destroyed because my hair was never meant to be chemically straightened. I tried to look like everyone else, and as a result, I have to rely on weaves or hair straighteners to have a good hair day now.

Changing my hair didn't magically make me fit in. School remained a battleground, but I gave the girls as good as I got.

When they stopped to glare at me as I passed, I'd pretend not to give a damn. 'What are youse lookin' at?' I'd say. All I really wanted was a quiet life, so I was mortified when my ma found out what was going on and got their parents involved. Oh God, I just wanted to keep my head down and to be left alone at that stage. I should have listened to my ma, who never wanted me to go to that school at all. She wanted the very best for Pariss and me, so she researched every school in the area. And she had wanted me to go somewhere else. But I wouldn't listen to her and went to the school I wanted to go to. Years later, I bumped into a few of the girls I fell out with, and they apologised for giving me a hard time. I'd never hold it against them. We were all kids, and kids do stupid and unkind things.

Still, I couldn't wait to get out of that school. After the leaving certificate, I joined Theatre Studies in Coláiste Dhúlaigh. I loved it and made some of the best friends of my life there. The three-year course covered stage management, production design, acting skills, dancing and singing. It was a tough course, and we worked long hours. Our project was to produce a commercially viable show for Christmas each year, with us dressed up as Disney characters. We had to design our costumes, create the stage set, find corporate sponsors, write the scripts and then travel around schools to stage our shows. We worked around the clock to meet our deadlines at times.

At the end of second year, I went on a J1 visa to San Diego, California. It was my first real experience of living and working away from home. I worked in Smyths toy store part-time while in college to raise some of the money to get to America, but the cost of the visa and eight flights amounted to more than my savings. Of course, it was Ma and Nanny who subsidised the rest of the trip. They were always there for me, encouraging me to spread my wings.

I travelled with others from college, and we moved into an apartment in Barclay Square. We should have known something was up when we managed to rent the apartment so easily. Not many American landlords were keen to hand over their properties to Irish students for three months.

Then we saw armed police officers leaping from a helicopter that landed outside our apartment as we made dinner one night, and it all became clear. The place was San Diego's answer to the Bronx: a crime-ridden area where cop sirens wailed all night. We learned that a woman was shot sixty times in the chest in our block just before we arrived. The estate agents were happy to accept Irish students as tenants because they couldn't find anyone else stupid enough to live there.

It wasn't easy to find jobs. My friend Karina and I walked the streets of San Diego hunting for work. It was 38 degrees Celsius outside, and we ended up looking like two balls of sweat knocking on doors, handing out our CVs. An Irish manager of a restaurant called Ruth's Chris Steakhouse finally took pity on us and gave us both jobs as hosts. Of course, finding work wasn't the end of our financial problems. We seemed to spend money a lot faster than we earned it, and there were regular calls home.

'Hi, Ma, yeah, the weather is great. Would you be able to sort me out with a loan until I get paid next week?'

Ma would eventually agree to send money before adding, 'Just don't be asking your nanny for money.'

The following week it would be: 'Hi, Nanny, yeah, we're having a great time. Would you be able to sub me a loan until I get paid next week?'

That call usually finished with the line: 'Can you do me another favour, Nanny? Don't tell Ma I called.'

After writing about all the financial hardships my ma and Nanny endured down the years, I realise that I sound like a spoilt brat. I've had so many experiences that were denied to them. Nanny and Ma never had the safety net of someone to help them out the way they helped me. It was much harder for them. Any time I was stuck, I had the comfort of knowing they were there for me. Oh my God, there were so many times when I don't know what I'd have done without them.

At the same time, I was never just handed money. I had to work and earn money and show I was making an effort as well. But I realise now that Pariss and I have had it easy in comparison. My ma sacrificed a lot to give me every chance, and not everything I did was worthy of those sacrifices.

As my friends and I made our way to and from our apartment most days, we passed a giant Mexican man who liked to loiter around his front door. He was fearsome looking. Built like a mountain, he had this towering height and a massive belly. We got to know him as Frank, and anytime I stopped to chat, I couldn't help noticing the bang of weed outside his door. The fumes were more powerful than Frank having the occasional toke at his door. Frank invited the Irish into his apartment one day, and sure enough, he had his own grow house inside. He filled every room with thriving cannabis plants.

'Would you like a smoke?' he asked, being a neighbourly sort, and what could we say? It would have been rude to turn down his hospitality.

It was all great until one of the lads from upstairs, who'd never smoked weed in his life, started dragging on a spliff like a lifelong pothead.

'Jesus, Mick, slow down!' I said, but it was too late. Within minutes, Mick went deadly quiet, turned pond green and then spewed like the demon from *The Exorcist*.

Getting into pubs or clubs was impossible in San Diego. The legal age for buying alcohol is twenty-one in America, and even though we all brought fake drivers' licences from Ireland, the doormen weren't fooled. Luckily, San Diego city is less than twenty miles from Mexico, where the bar owners were less concerned about the age of their customers.

At least once a week, we'd catch the San Diego trolley, an electric light-rail train like the Luas, to the border. After presenting our passports, we'd walk over to the Mexican side and then run, as fast as we could, to a taxi. We'd all cram in and order the driver not to stop until he got us to our favourite dingy haunt. Tijuana had a bustling nightlife, but it also ranked as one of the top five most dangerous and most murderous cities globally. It was riddled with drug trafficking, organised crime, kidnappings and car jackings.

I felt a familiar sense of relief after we left Mexico one night and waited for the trolley on the American side of the border. Everything felt safer there. The trolley arrived, and as we boarded, someone grabbed me from behind by the scruff of the neck. I let out a scream as I was dragged backwards off the train. My heart pounded even harder when I realised the assailants were San Diego police. Another scuffle was going on behind me, and I realised the police were also wrestling with David, a good friend of mine from Colaiste Dhulaigh. I looked up and could see the wide eyes of the other passengers on the trolley staring at the unfolding scene.

'What the hell?' I cried. I'd never been more scared in my life. 'What's going on, David?' A million things were running through my mind. Had someone planted drugs on us? Had we inadvertently become drug mules? Life in a maximum-security prison flashed before my eyes. Oh my God, what were Ma and Nanny going to say?

The reality was all a bit more mundane. It turned out David and I had been smoking cigarettes too close to the trolley, and we were supposed to be standing further back. Big red signs were hanging everywhere, but we never saw them until the police pointed them out. To make matters worse, we'd chucked our butts on the ground before boarding. I'd never litter like that now, but we were young and stupid then. We were charged for multiple offences and given a court date.

Ma was outraged when she heard I'd got a court summons. Furious. 'Don't you come home without sorting that out!' she warned, even though we had no intention of skipping the court date. We were afraid of our lives that we'd be forever banned from the United States if we didn't turn up. Everything is so much more dramatic and urgent when you're young.

We expected to get a fine, but instead, we were ordered to write letters of apology, which were read out in court before the judge. Whenever my nanny hears about San Diego, the first thing she talks about is the time I was 'nearly jailed in America'. I don't think she'll ever get over it.

I had three great years in Coláiste Dhúlaigh, and I made lifelong friends there. My compulsive cleanliness and the constant showering continued right through my late teens and into my twenties. I was still showering three times a day then, and friends used to slag me for my obsession with clean runners.

I have never grown out of it, really. I don't shower like

that now, but I'm constantly brushing my teeth and washing around me all the time. I clean my car three times a week. This morning, I brought my nanny a latte, her favourite drink since she discovered it last year. But I didn't sit down with her. I went around cleaning while she slurped her latte, saying, 'They didn't make coffee like that back in my day, Jade.' My surroundings are spotless, but I don't see it as a bad thing. My logic is: clean house, clean mind. It helps me think more clearly and work more efficiently if there is no clutter or dirt around me. I swear, I'm not like that when I'm in someone else's house or a hotel room. I don't go around running my finger along window sills checking for dust. I'm relaxed in anyone else's space, but I'm just a happier person when my own surroundings are tidy and clean.

I realise I'm like my mother in that sense — she has to have everything immaculate and is always cleaning too. While writing this book and talking to Nanny, I've learned that Larry was like that too. It's in the blood.

The only problem with Coláiste Dhúlaigh was that I didn't do my homework before I went there. My course was an academic one involving a lot of theory and the practice of theatre rather than performance and drama. We had only one dance class and one singing class a week, so I was deluded to think I'd be ready to start auditions afterwards. I still needed proper discipline and training in the craft of acting when I graduated. The Lir Academy in Trinity, which provides professional training for actors, didn't exist then. I don't know if it would have mattered anyway, because my dream was always to go to London. I thought London would be the making of me.

There were no Irish actors or people on the TV who represented how I looked, so I thought I'd never get a job in film, TV or theatre in Ireland. I saw lots of Black or mixed-race people in the English soaps, but no one looked like me in *Fair City*. The only person from Ireland who looked like me was Samantha Mumba, who was making it big in America then. I had no interest in going back to America – I don't think that even crossed my mind.

For me, London was on my doorstep and seemed like this massive multicultural city where I would blend in. Ma had brought us over a lot when we were younger, so I reckoned London would be a far better fit for me than Dublin. I would be accepted there and would have a better chance of working in the performing arts. There has been a massive shift in Ireland since, but back then, I believed there was nothing for me – a mixed-race aspiring actor – in Ireland. That's why I wanted to go.

So, after a few months of saving money, I made the big announcement to my best friend, Fiona: 'I'm moving to London in two weeks.'

Fiona was stunned. She knew I was thinking of going, but when you're young, you say these things, and she probably thought that I'd never go at all. I had applied for and been accepted on a drama course at Buckinghamshire New University but had no plane ticket, no accommodation and nothing arranged for this big move. I still had it in my head that I was going, and that was it.

Fiona broke down in tears. 'You can't go! We're the best off friends. What am I going to do?'

Fiona and I had been inseparable since we'd met in primary school. We also went to secondary school together, and when the rest of the girls were mad into chasing boys, we were happy to enjoy each other's company. We'd go dancing and shopping together, and we always had such a laugh. When we were sixteen and seventeen, we used to go to a club called Heaven in Blanchardstown. I used my ma's passport as ID by changing the date of birth with an erasable black marker. It helped that my ma looked about twelve in her passport photo, but if the doorman had just rubbed his finger over the date, it would have come off on his hand.

Ma was OK about me going to clubs if she could drop me off and collect me. She'd even let my friends and me have a drink in the house as long as she could supervise and all the other parents agreed. She was strict without being a complete killjoy. But she and Fiona's parents refused to let us go on a sixth-year holiday. When everyone else was going to Magaluf or Santa Ponsa to celebrate the leaving cert, Fiona and I had to stay home. Our parents promised we could go away the next year when we were both eighteen instead. Fiona and I saved like mad, and our parents helped out, and we went to live in Ibiza for a month the following summer. Like, who goes to stay on an expensive island like Ibiza for a month?

Ibiza is all about the glamorous clubs and parties, and we spent a fortune on a ticket that admitted us into two of these super clubs. By the time our hotly anticipated big night arrived, I had an ear infection and Fiona had a kidney infection. We lasted about an hour in the clubs before we had to go home.

The nightclubs were out of our budget, so instead, we found an Irish bar where we drank Sex on the Beach cocktails every night. Cocktails are lethal. We should have had one and moved onto something less potent, but we didn't know that. We'd try to drink them all night, and we'd end up vomiting all the way home. I'm sure the barmen saw us coming. *Oh, no, here are these two gobshites again. Do they ever learn?*

For most of our lives, Fiona and I had gone everywhere together. So, when I told her I was off to London in a fortnight, she was gutted. I was only home an hour that evening when she called me.

'I told my mam and dad – I'm coming with you,' she said.

Through Fiona's sister, we managed to contact a man who rented properties in London. We secured a bedsit in the centre of London at a price we could barely afford. Then we bought the cows in a bag shop in town. I've never seen cases as big before or since. We were determined not to leave anything behind us.

'We're going to London, and we're never coming back!' we said to each other countless times. We never said that within hearing of our families, but that was our intent. We were glad to be getting out of Dublin in 2009. The country was in an economic depression, and the news was full of doom and gloom, banking scandals, job losses, negative equity and property values collapsing. The UK economy was also at its weakest in thirty years, but London was relatively unscathed. We knew it wouldn't be hard to find jobs there.

Fiona and I weren't completely stupid. We knew that the cows were overweight as we left for the airport. It took three of us to lift mine into my mother's boot. I had packed more than twenty pairs of shoes alone because I couldn't bear to leave anything.

'Seriously, girls, where do you think you're going with those bags?' Fiona's dad said.

Our parents were secretly laughing at us.

'We'll just pay the few extra quid,' I said breezily. 'It can't be that much.'

It came as a shock to us when the check-in woman refused point-blank to accept our bags at all. It wasn't a case of paying extra; our bags were not going in the hold of that Ryanair plane.

'This case is sixty kilos alone,' she said. 'The bag handlers won't be able to lift this on or off the carousel. Do you realise that's nine and a half stone in weight? Plenty of adults weigh less than that bag!'

Fiona and I looked at each other in desperation. Then we looked to our parents, who could only offer smug 'I-told-you-so' expressions. Nanny was the clever one who'd anticipated the problem and provided the only solution. She pulled out a roll of plastic bags from her handbag and started peeling them off.

'Start taking out the stuff you don't need,' she said. 'We'll bring your things home.'

So Fiona and I got onto the airport terminal floor and started tearing through our cows, all the while bemoaning what we had to leave behind. We were going for life, so we needed everything. I had stilettos, puffer jackets, and if I owned a feather boa, it would have been in there too. We couldn't bear leaving a piece of any outfit behind. But we stuffed Nanny's plastic bags anyway, and after removing over half of the contents of our cases, we were still overweight. I had to fork out fifty euros extra to check my bag.

Finally, we headed towards the security gates, ready to get our trip underway. After all the laughter and the drama over the luggage, the tears started flowing. Nanny had to walk away because she was crying so hard. She calls me her treasure, and she is so precious to me too. We are unbelievably close. If she's sick, I'll know about it, even if there are a thousand miles between us. That's just how we work.

I think it must be like the relationship she had with her father because there's an understanding and unconditional love between us. I've often wondered if her father had survived, would everything have been different for Nanny? If their relationship was like ours, it would have been indestructible. I know there's nothing I could do, or Nanny could do, that could tear us apart.

Leaving Nanny behind was the most heartbreaking part for me. Ma and I have an unbreakable bond, but she is forever young to me. Ma is my best friend, we dance together, go shopping together and go to concerts and gigs together. I knew she would be a regular visitor to London. She's my rock who never grows older.

But I worry about Nanny. She's more vulnerable because of her age, and I know she's not going to be around forever. She's such a caring and kind-hearted person that even the neighbours call her 'mother nature'. When I was a child, she was always this protective buffer between Ma and me. She'd cover for me when I mitched from school because, as far as Nanny is concerned, the sun shines out of my backside. She still cherishes the pink bunny rabbit she bought me the day I was born thirty-two years ago. She always says that we were inseparable from the minute I arrived. 'Like two peas in a pod,' she says.

Ma had to work a lot when we were children, so I spent a

lot of time with Nanny. When I think about it, Nanny worked long hours when her own children were small, so she probably had the relationship with me that she never had the time to have with my ma. They always say that the first grandchild is a bit closer to their grandparents anyway, don't they? There's just this bond there that will never disappear. I didn't want to leave her, but I thought, *If I don't do this now, I'll never do it.* Fiona was bawling too, and her mam and dad were in tears.

When we reached security, Fiona and I looked at each other and started laughing because we had what we call 'panda eye' from the crying. Our eyes were like coal pits, and streaks of black mascara ran down our faces.

I remember the day we left Dublin so well. I was convinced that was it for me: once I landed in London, I would be discovered and become a world-renowned actress like my idol, Cate Blanchett. I was certain to enter the pantheon of great Irish heroes like Brenda Fricker.

So was it any wonder that I cried so much the day I left Dublin? After all, it was the end of an era. I was never coming back, never living with Nanny and Ma again. I was heading for the Hollywood Walk of Fame after a quick pitstop in London. It still makes me laugh when I think back. I'd no idea. Some would describe me as naïve, and others would say I was a dreamer. I'd probably say I was completely deluded.

DRAMA SCHOOL

If we'd had any sense, we would have bought regular suitcases on wheels. Instead, we were forced to lug our cows along a hot and humid London road filled with people, traffic, noise and fumes. We were completely lost.

'For fuck's sake, we're walking around in circles!' I cried. 'Where is this bloody place?'

Everything had gone well until we'd emerged from Caledonian Road underground station. We had an address for the bedsit on Caledonian Road, but the sequence of numbers on the road didn't make any sense. I know it wasn't that long ago, but we hadn't even heard of Google Maps then. We also didn't realise that Caledonian Road is a mile and a half long and runs right through the inner London borough of Islington. We were tired, sweaty and despairing, and then we heard a voice.

'Oy! Aww you the two gels from Dublan?' The landlord, Mario, had been waiting in the flat for us, and he was about to leave when he spotted us on the road. 'This is your plyce 'ere,' he said.

We were so grateful to see him that we could have

kissed him. The house was just south of Caledonian Road underground, an area popular with the waves of Irish immigrants in the 1950s.

It turned out our flat was in the attic of an old Georgian terraced house that had been turned into bedsits. We had to drag the cows up three flights of impossibly narrow stairs. We hadn't expected spaciousness when we'd agreed to rent a bedsit, but we were still taken aback when Mario opened the door. There was a tiny kitchenette with a hob and fridge to the right, a standard double bed and wardrobe to the left and a window onto the street facing us. Our new home was even more miniature than we'd imagined.

Either the house's foundations or the joists under the floorboards had sunk because the floor was angled at an extreme slant. Everything tended to slide down the floorboards towards the kitchenette.

Mario showed us the shared bathroom on the landing, and Fiona and I recoiled with 'ugh!' faces. We're house-proud people. We like everything to be spotless, and this bathroom was pee-soaked and filthy. We had to share it with an actor in one bedsit and an old guy, who always had a bang of drink off him, in the other. Neither were bothered about cleanliness, so it was left to us to clean the toilet. Oh, it was nasty, but Fiona and I continued to live in that bedsit and share that same double bed for the next two years.

Our priority after arriving was to find jobs because we

had no money. I had only two hundred pounds or so leaving Dublin, and I'd forked out a quarter of those savings to the check-in agent at the airport for my overweight cow.

I wasn't picky or choosy; I didn't care if it was scrubbing floors or washing dishes. I would do anything. My nanny is an absolute grafter, and Ma always had a million and one jobs. They were both among a group of women from Whitestown Drive who used to work for big catering events around the country. Ma always had a full-time job, but at nights and weekends, she and Nanny used to do catering work for people like tycoon businessman Tony O'Reilly on his Castlemartin estate in Kildare. Or they'd work for Punchestown Racecourse or golf clubs like St Anne's in Clontarf. Nanny was a kitchen porter doing the pot wash, and Ma did the waitressing. As soon as I got older, I was roped in as a waitress too. I had skills to support myself in university, and I had no problem using them.

Fiona and I raced frantically around London for the next few days seeking work and a UK National Insurance number. By the end of the week, Fiona had secured a position in a beauty salon, and I'd got a job at the retail store French Connection.

We couldn't afford a TV, so our entertainment was to sit at the open window, chain-smoking and surveying our kingdom below. The Cally, as Caledonian Road was locally known, was a busy central London artery. There wasn't much around us in terms of restaurants and shopping apart from a twenty-four-hour shop and a Centra. A few nice lads ran the Centra, and Fiona and I left our apartment keys with them if we were both going out. Yes, we shared a single set of keys. Why didn't we go out and get another set cut? I have no idea.

The tube station was right beside us, and people poured in and out day and night. Our next-door neighbours were the occupants of Pentonville Prison, a category B men's jail from the 1840s. Fun fact: Oscar Wilde and Eamon de Valera spent time in the place, and poor Roger Casement was hanged from the gallows there.

The Cally was also a busy site for sex workers to ply their trade. We watched a stream of cars slowing down and pulling up and deals being struck and broken. We saw rows and brawls and near murder going on some nights. After a while, a friend donated an old TV to us, but even though we turned and twisted the aerial in every direction, all we got was a snowy flicker on the screen. We returned to smoking our brains out at the window. Nanny and Ma visited whenever they could. Nanny was just like us: she sat at the window mesmerised by everything going on outside. All of London life went on right below us.

If I compare our living standards with those that Nanny and Mam endured, our surroundings were palatial. But by modern standards, they were grim. Even though our flat was tiny, people would still come to stay with us. We'd get out the air mattress and stretch it out at the bottom of our bed. We were lucky if we had bread and cheese for a toasted sandwich. Sometimes, toast was all we had to offer people who visited.

We were always stuck for money, and we were too proud to ask for help by then. We thought of ourselves as independent working women in London, but some of our money-saving antics were daft. I remember how we rushed home from work in January 2010 to pack for a flight to Ireland. It was snowing, and many flights were being delayed or cancelled. Still, Fiona and I hoped to make it to our friend Mairead's twenty-first party in Dublin. We wanted to shower before we left, but I turned the tap in the bathroom and heard a gurgle. Nothing happened.

'What do you mean the shower's not working?'

'I mean, there's no water coming out of the showerhead.'

'Oh my God, what are we going to do now?'

What could we do? We averted disaster by washing ourselves using the plastic basin in the kitchen sink. But then we discovered another calamity – we were out of perfume. We felt naked without a generous spritz of scent, but the perfume bottle was empty, and we hadn't any spare cash to replace it.

'Air freshener!' I said.

'Air freshener?'

Anytime we entered that grimy bathroom on the landing, we always armed ourselves with a lavender Tesco Air

Freshener. I've no idea why it had to be lavender. We could have bought lemon or white linen – why would we pick an old-lady smell like lavender?

'I'll spray it in the air, and you walk through the haze, and then you spray it in the air for me.'

Fiona and I felt very clever, like a regular pair of geniuses. Then we walked through the airport duty-free a couple of hours later and saw any amount of beautiful perfumes to sample. Then we felt like a right pair of dopes.

We were always smashed. The trouble was that we didn't earn a lot, and much of our money went into paying the rent and buying the travel card. That didn't stop us from having a social life, though. Money was tight, but we always scraped enough together to party and go for pints. Those two years on the Caledonian Road were among the best of our lives. It was our first bit of freedom, and we loved having our own flat and a sense of independence.

One by one, all our friends moved over to London too. Two weeks after Fiona and I moved to London, Karina, my best friend in Coláiste Dhúlaigh, arrived. She spent a night renting in Kentish town before discovering she was sharing the place with bedbugs. She moved into our bed that night and ended up staying with us for over a month. With Karina in town, our social life went mental. A year later, Fiona's sister Ciara moved over. In the end, no one from our circle was left in Dublin. We were all over in London and having the craic.

I started my three-year degree course in drama and musical theatre the month after we arrived in London and discovered, once again, that I hadn't done my research. The commute to the university in Buckinghamshire was long and expensive, and the course was theory-based again. It wasn't what I'd expected. Within months, I left and joined a few part-time courses in acting and musical theatre.

Ma nearly had a heart attack when she heard I had dropped out. 'Attending that university was the whole point of you going to London!'

'It's the wrong course. I've looked into it now, and I need to apply for drama school.'

'Drama school? How much is that going to cost?'

I gulped before telling her. It was a shock to me when I learned the cost of attending a drama school in London. I tried them all, and the fees were similar. 'We're talking twenty-five grand in fees over two years.'

'What? Are you joking me, Jade? We can't afford that!'

'I know, but I think if I worked two jobs and saved like mad for a couple of years, I could raise the money.'

My ma sighed. 'You're not going to be able to raise that much money,' she said. 'If it's what you really want to do, I'll get a loan to add to your savings.'

For the next two years, I worked and saved money, and my mother took out a credit union loan, so I could attend my dream course. The plan was to emerge industry-ready and fully trained within two years. It turned out to be a nightmare. I won't name the school, but I hated it.

Singing was my first love. I loved dance and drama, but singing was my favourite. I don't claim to be a virtuoso like Whitney Houston or Mariah Carey, but let's say I knew I could hold a note. The principal of this school also taught all the singing classes. For two solid years, he told me that I wasn't good enough. He was short and stout with tightly cropped hair and liked to wear polo necks, and it seemed to be a constant source of joy to him to jeer his students.

'You're so lazy. You're not trying. You have to work harder.' 'You lot are the worst year of students I've ever had – you are bone idle.' 'You're so stiff; it's like watching a block of wood ...' He was like a broken record player, saying the same thing over and over again.

We staged three shows or productions a year, but I never got the opportunity to shine. I can't even remember the roles I had because I've blocked out all those experiences. I really have. No matter how small a role I had, I always got great feedback from everyone else. I always got praise for my performances even if they were small. The principal even had to admit I was 'watchable' – the only decent thing he had to say about me.

But I was constantly shoved down and pushed back by him, told that I couldn't handle this or that part and I was lucky to get a small role in the background. He had his favourites, the ones that he liked to place in the spotlight all the time. And that was fine, but he made out I was the weakest link in the class. I was always being told I wasn't good enough.

As a performer, part of the job is to learn to handle criticism. But his running commentary was destructive criticism, never constructive. It came to a point after the first year where I felt really anxious and ended up on antidepressants for months. Drama school was horrendous, and I needed medication just to help me face the day in college.

One day we were all asked to pose for a promo photo to advertise the college. At the time, I was the first person of colour to attend the school. 'Jade, look! I've put you at the front to show we're an ethnic college,' he laughed, and he thought it was a great joke.

I look back and think, fucking hell, that was really inappropriate; why didn't I challenge that? Why didn't I say something? I don't think it hit home at the time. I was a people-pleaser, and I lacked so much confidence then. I don't think I was capable of confronting him about using me like that.

And to be honest, I felt lucky to get into drama school at all. I was desperate to learn. I appreciated being there and wouldn't do anything to jeopardise that. So many people audition to get in, and so few manage to get a place. Everyone struggles in drama school because it's hard work. You're ripping yourself apart to become a different character, and you're killing yourself to pay for the school. All my classmates were juggling multiple jobs to keep going. And that was how it was for me.

Once I got my place, I was determined to keep it, even if it meant working day and night to pay for it. I got to the college at 6 a.m. to work as a cleaner. After classes, I'd head for my second job as an usher and front-of-house in a theatre. On weekends, I had a waitressing job during the day, and I'd work until nearly midnight some nights in the theatre. It was a tough time, but it was tough for all of us.

When it came near the end of second year, the students had to work on CVs and fill out forms for Spotlight and actors' agents. One of the forms contained a simple ethnicity box-ticking exercise to identify ourselves for potential employers.

There were lots of boxes and options.

'White English', 'white Welsh', 'white Scottish' or 'white Irish'?

'Black', 'mixed-race', 'mixed Caribbean', 'mixed African' or 'mixed Asian'?

'Indian', 'Pakistani', 'Bangladeshi', 'Chinese' or 'Arab'?

There was a huge selection of identities to choose from. I ticked my usual box. Our dance teacher went through our forms, and then she called me over. She was a bit hesitant and clearly confused. 'Jade, why have you ticked 'white Irish'?' she asked.

How do you explain that? Up until then, I'd always

struggled with these ethnicity boxes in Ireland because the only way to identify as Irish was to tick the 'white Irish' box. Obviously, I knew I wasn't white, but there was never a box to accommodate 'mixed-race' or 'Black Irish'. It was like we didn't exist. It always made absolute sense to me to tick the 'white Irish' box.

'You can't describe yourself as 'white Irish' when your headshot shows that you're dark-skinned with curly hair,' she said. 'No one looking for a white Irish actor will hire you.'

Of course, I understood what she was saying. But it was the box I ticked all my life. I never wanted to lose my Irish identity. I wonder why I never thought of asking, 'why isn't there a Black Irish box?' I never did. I had to process what she said for a minute or two. 'So what box *do* I tick?' I asked.

'You're mixed-race, so tick the 'mixed-race' box. It will open up a whole new range of roles you could be cast in.'

So that's what I did. I didn't have any emotional reaction to it. I realised then how daft I was ticking that box in terms of my career. I look back now, and it makes me laugh. That poor teacher must have thought I was bloody blind to describe myself as 'white Irish'. It's mad, but I couldn't see that until that day. That was the first time my identity became 'mixed-race'.

The day arrived when I was called for my first ever audition after finishing drama school and my first West End audition – a production of the *Lion King* in the West End. No pressure, so. The roles of Nala and an ensemble cast were up for grabs in what's referred to as 'a dance call'. After drama school, I didn't have a lot of confidence anyway, and it didn't help when I arrived that day and realised how many people were auditioning. Hundreds of us were crammed into one long hallway.

I started to feel the fear of God when I saw some of the girls doing the splits and stretching their legs past their ears. There was no conversation in the place – apart from me, of course. I had my usual dose of verbal diarrhoea. *Jayz, this place is packed, isn't it? Wonder how long this is going to take? Oh my God, you've very flexible, aren't you?* Everyone was so deadly serious and focused on their warm-ups that it was like I didn't exist. This was do or die for everyone in the hall.

The casting crew drove us into a big studio first and started the elimination process by having us jog round and round the room. The *Lion King* is a very technical production, and I guess they wanted to find people who were light on their feet and balletic in their movements. We jogged while they whispered and pointed, and their beady eyes watched everyone's posture, stance and athleticism. We were like cattle being herded around a sales mart. Then the director started jabbing a pointy finger and yelling, 'You, cut! You, cut! Cut! Cut! Cut!' Joggers were being stopped in their tracks and exiting the room at speed. God, my heart was thumping.

The jogging rounds ended, and the herd was much thinned as we entered the next round. This time they had us doing ballet positions. I'm sure everyone could hear my heart banging at that stage, but I'd barely raised my foot off the ground when I saw the pointy finger aimed at me. 'Cut!' the casting director yelled, and I slunk out of the room and packed up in the hall with everyone else.

My love for musical theatre had faded away in drama school, and this audition experience was just another nail in the coffin for me.

Drama school was hard. It's only all these years later that I realise how much I've been able to achieve once I had the opportunity to shine. But back then, I never got the opportunity to be the best I could be and, for a brief time, I got depressed about it. But eventually I was able to come off the antidepressants after a few months and soldiered on. I didn't want to be dependent on pills to make myself feel better. The rose-tinted glasses were gone, though, and I felt a mass of insecurities about performing.

Most actors dream of becoming famous, but I also just wanted to work and do what I love and get paid for it. That's all I still want to do, but I left drama school with no confidence. All the spark and the joy I felt about performance was extinguished. I fell out of love with singing and haven't sung a note since. I went to drama school with a dream of working in musical theatre, and shortly after I finished, I rang my ma, and I said, 'I've decided I don't want to do musical theatre anymore.'

I'm not stupid. I know I'm very privileged. It's only while writing this book that I learned my ma worked after school so she could afford drama classes. Who knows, if she had had the same opportunities she afforded me, maybe she could have gone down a different path and become an actor? Instead, I was the one lucky enough to get the opportunities.

So can you imagine her reaction? She had taken out a big loan from the credit union in both our names to fund me through drama school. That was back in 2012, and honest to God, that loan is only coming to an end this year. My ma had done so much to help me realise my dream to work in musical theatre, and here I was telling her I'd changed my mind and didn't want to do it anymore.

I can still hear her: 'Are you kidding me, Jade? Are you actually kidding me?'

LOVE

I wouldn't have survived drama school at all if it wasn't for Tom's love and support. He kept reminding me why I'd started in the first place – my love for performing. When I felt broken and at rock bottom, he picked up the pieces and urged me to keep doing my best.

They say first impressions are critical, yet when Tom and I met, he thought I was plain rude, and I barely noticed him. We first met about four or five months after I moved to England, while I was still in university. I was working on the floor in French Connection when some guy approached me asking for the manager. I didn't pay much attention and indicated with a jerk of my head. 'Down there,' I said and continued organising the clothes rails.

He immediately thought I was abrupt and bad-mannered.

I didn't learn of that encounter and about Tom's first impression of me until much later, of course. Tom was there that day for a job interview, and he started on the floor a week or so later. He was such a handsome man. Tall and rangy, he had soft chocolate-brown eyes, tightly shorn thick brown hair and a neat beard. I don't know how I failed to notice him the first time I saw him because I was obsessed with him from the day he started. I remember going home after his first day and saying to Fiona, 'Oh my God, there's this new boy at work …' Every day, I'd wreck her head with Tom-said-this and Tom-did-that. Seriously, it got to the stage where if I mentioned his name, Fiona threatened to belt me one.

As romances go, this was a slow burner. I thought he was stunning, but it took a while for him to warm to me. I think it takes people time to get me because I have a very dry sense of humour. I don't think he knew what to make of me at first.

We got to know each other slowly, as colleagues and then friends. I learned that he wasn't long out of a relationship, so I felt I couldn't make my feelings for him apparent. My bedsit on the Cally was not far from his home, so Tom showed me a bus route that was nearly a quarter the price of taking the tube to work. We started taking the bus home together every day. Some days we'd get off the bus and sit at the stop for hours, talking about nothing. We'd sit there chatting, oblivious to the freezing cold and lashing rain, clearly not wanting to leave each other. But still, Tom didn't make a move.

After a while, we started meeting up to go for walks and coffee. Tom lived beside the Angel, a historic landmark and area in Islington in the city centre. Tom was a true Londoner whose family had lived in the heart of the city for generations. He didn't have a Cockney accent, but his accent was distinctly

London. He introduced me to pie and mash shops, which have been feeding working-class Londoners for centuries. These small family-run shops, some in the same hands for generations, are still found in the East End and South London. The traditional places had ancient wooden pews as seats and walls decorated in green and white Victorian tiles.

They serve up beef pies swimming in 'liquor', a nuclear-green-coloured parsley sauce. I drew the line at eating jellied eels, another traditional Londoners' dish because it was the only fish that could survive the pollution in the Thames. Tom liked to scoff this slimy delicacy, but only on a day out at the beach. Yes, most of us love an ice cream at the seaside, but Tom enjoyed a jellied eel. A good feed of homemade pie, with a flaky pastry topping, mash and liquor cost about a fiver, and the food was delicious.

We were an unlikely couple in some ways because we were complete opposites. He was so much quieter than me, but he was good humoured and quick to smile, and he made me laugh all the time.

We also shared a passion for fashion and an obsession with clothes and style. Tom was even more fastidious than me, ironing everything down to his boxers. Whenever he went to sit, he'd hold out his shirt or top and then arrange it and smooth it around him so it wouldn't crease while sitting. How many men do you know who'd do that? He was always pristine.

We remained friends for a long time, six months or more, even though we were finding more and more excuses to spend time together. One night, a group of us went to our local, the Grand Union bar on Upper Street in Islington. Tom and I left the others at the table and went outside to have a cigarette. There was such a chemistry between us that night, I could have almost touched it. As we turned to return to the pub, we paused, stared into each other's eyes and kissed. He says I instigated it; I say it was him. Either way, it was bound to happen. After we kissed, that was it: we were a couple for the next nine years.

I fell headlong in love after that. He was perfect, always making these wild romantic gestures. I remember receiving a text message on my way out of drama school one day. The text told me to cross the road to the pub, look in the window and find the first in a series of clues in a romantic treasure hunt. The Post-it note there told me where to find the next one. I followed the trail and found about six more Post-it notes, and then I got fed up and rang him.

'For God's sake, where am I supposed to be going?' I demanded. 'Just tell me!'

I had no patience. He had gone to the trouble of placing Post-it notes around the city in places that were meaningful in our relationship. It must have taken him ages to put the whole treasure hunt together, and I wanted to end it after a handful of clues. He made me persevere. Eventually, I got to the last Post-it, which led to a picnic in the summer sunshine in a quiet Georgian garden park. I mean, how lovely was that?

While I had decided to give up Musical Theatre, I knew acting was for me and so I did a lot of work performing after finishing drama school, but it was unpaid voluntary work. The work usually involved profit-share gigs in small theatres above pubs. I'd end up working two or three weeks on a show with nine or ten other people and, depending on how many tickets were sold, I might walk away with twenty pounds. Profit share was not very profitable. It was all about building up a CV after getting out of drama school. Meanwhile, I held down several jobs in retail and waitressing to pay the bills. There were many times when I said, 'I can't do this anymore.' It was Tom who encouraged me and urged me to remember my dream.

It's safe to say that I doubted my choices at times. I wondered if maybe I'd made a big mistake and performing arts wasn't the career for me. I guess self-doubt is something that goes through every actor's head at different points. Rejection is part of the job, and the casting process shoots holes in every actor's confidence. Acting and instability go hand in hand, so sometimes you feel like tearing your hair out.

I continued to run around London, attending audition after audition, but it seemed I was getting nowhere. It was little wonder when I think about it. Drama school had ripped out any confidence I had, and I'd left feeling shit about myself. I had no self-belief; how did I expect anyone else to believe in me?

I heard about a TV and film course in Bow Street Academy, the national screen-acting school in Dublin. Everything I heard was good. *Maybe it would help if I did that course?* I thought. Something had to work for me. I decided to take a chance, do some training in Dublin and try to turn my luck around.

My new schedule involved flying to Dublin every Sunday night to attend the Bow Street course for two days. Then it was straight back to London on Wednesday, where I worked two jobs. I used my cheeriest voice for a position in a call centre for an eight-hour day. Then I wore a server's apron to work in Pizza Express in the West End until midnight. The restaurant was busy and buzzy, full of theatregoers every evening. I often turned heads with my Dublin accent, especially when I served Irish diners. 'Jesus, you don't look Irish, but you sure sound it!' they'd say. There were times when I felt I should be offended. *What is an Irish person supposed to look like exactly?* But mostly, I was too busy to feel anything.

After months of working in London and training in Dublin, I was exhausted and falling asleep on my feet. I spent the night before my end of year project in Bow Street lying on the bathroom floor and puking into the toilet bowl. My final exam scene involved me playing Halle Berry's role in the movie *Losing Isaiah*. The film is about a former crack-addicted mother battling to retrieve the baby she'd abandoned in a dumpster.

I can safely say that my illness informed my work that day. My eyes were blood-red slits, and my skin was grey. I looked and felt the part of a desperate recovering drug addict. I did my piece to camera in one take and caught the plane back to London. It was a crazy schedule, but it worked. Attending Bow Street began to help open doors for me in both England and Ireland.

Before going to Bow Street, my agent submitted me for roles, but I rarely got auditions. Once I started meeting more people through the college, things started to happen for me. I was introduced to a few casting directors who began calling me for parts. Maybe casting directors didn't know I existed before, but suddenly I was getting auditions, and I was getting auditions in Ireland for the first time. I was happy; it was progress.

My first acting job in London was with Shane Meadows, one of the best directors in the world. It was deadly because he is also one of my favourite directors of all time. I remember arriving petrified on the set of his TV series *The Virtues*. I was hired to play a hospital doctor in a feature-length episode, and I was shaking because I still harboured doubts about being an actor.

But the set was calm, really chilled, and everyone made

me feel at home. It gave me the confidence to throw myself into the role and become this new character. I discovered I loved the experience. I hadn't felt so happy since attending performing arts school as a kid. A huge weight lifted off my shoulders as I realised I am doing what I'm meant to be doing! This is what I want to do for the rest of my life! It was thrilling.

In the end, it was one of those gigs where if you blink you'll miss me. There was more of me on the cutting-room floor than there was in The Virtues, but I don't care because my name is still in the credits of a Shane Meadows series.

Every job I have done since, I've loved. I am telling somebody else's story. There's a responsibility to that but also a great sense of excitement, creativity and freedom. I get to leave my routine and my life behind for a brief time and transform myself into another person in another world. It's the ultimate form of escapism, and I revel in it. I'm an adult who is getting paid to play at being something or someone else; how much fun is that? I spent a long time thinking that musical theatre was the direction for me, but I've realised acting is my true passion after all.

Tom and I loved travelling, and every chance we got, we took off on city breaks. We stopped buying each other Christmas and birthdays presents and saved for foreign adventures instead. We travelled around Thailand one summer, and by the summer of 2018, we'd decided it was time to go again.

This time we decided to backpack around South East Asia for three months.

It was bliss to feel the balmy, tropical air on my skin as we got off the plane in Hanoi in Vietnam. As we stood at the carousel waiting to collect our luggage, I saw several missed calls on my phone from my London agent. I called her while we waited, wondering what she could want.

'You got the part!' she cried with delight. 'Jade, you got the part in the Roddy Doyle film!'

Before I'd left, I had auditioned for a small role in the movie Rosie in Dublin. The screenplay was about a family made homeless after losing their rented house. I was astonished to get the audition, but I never expected to get the role. So the news from my agent was like a bombshell. The part was small, but I was bleedin' delighted with myself. I nearly danced around the airport.

Then it hit me. I'm in Vietnam. I was in the middle of a bustling airport on the far side of the world, and filming was about to start in Ireland in six days. There was no chance the film would pay for me to fly home because the role of Megan wasn't a huge one. And the short notice meant that the flight back to Dublin would cost a small fortune. Tom and I didn't have that kind of cash because we were on a tight budget.

'Oh shit!' I said. 'It's a Roddy Doyle movie, and everything he does is phenomenal. What am I going to do?'

The film was an opportunity that I couldn't turn down, and

a part in a Roddy Doyle movie was a credit I couldn't afford to lose on my CV. I decided to get the money from somewhere. As usual, I turned to my family for help and promised I'd pay them all back as soon as I could. Even as I write this, I'm struck by how lucky I am to have the support of a great family. Knowing what I know now about my nanny, in particular, I realise how hard it must have been to struggle without any of that support.

So I was able to fly back to Dublin, shoot the film and return to Vietnam three days later. After that, I exhaled and began to absorb the charms of South East Asia. Tom and I travelled through the Mekong Delta's winding waterways, wandered in the lush hills of the Da Bac area, soaked in the stunning scenery of Cat Ba island and basked in the serenity of the Buddhist monasteries. It felt like an incredible luxury to be able to sit, think and listen. We travelled on to Cambodia, Malaysia, the Philippines and Indonesia.

By the time the three months were up, I felt refreshed and revitalised. I had shed all my stressors. We arrived back in London, and I took one long look at the clamour and the hectic pace of life around me.

'Nope,' I said. 'I'm not doing this anymore.' I realised that London was done for me. I was never surer of anything in my entire life. I was getting out of London.

VILLAGE LIFE

It never dawned on me until recently how Nanny, Ma and I all followed such a similar path in life. We all went to London, and we all felt the tug of some invisible thread to come home again.

The mysterious pull to return to Ireland seemed to take Nanny by surprise. She can't even explain it to this day. My ma couldn't get to London fast enough, yet she still returned. I swore I was never coming back, and here I was, suddenly contemplating a return to Dublin too.

Everyone knows London is one of the busiest cities in the world. For years, that buzz energised me, but suddenly I found it draining. I was wrecked running around like a headless chicken, and I remember calling Ma and telling her I was ready to come home and be minded for a while. I realised I needed a radical change in my life.

To be honest, I think the idea started percolating in my mind after returning to Dublin for a close family friend Noel's funeral the year before. I couldn't afford a flight, so I took the boat like my nanny and ma before me. Bloody hell, it was an eight-hour trip, but it turned out to be an important journey in more ways than one. Noel's wake and the funeral was such an eye-opener for me.

From the minute I arrived home, I was overwhelmed by how much everyone in Whitestown and further afield came together as a community. The doorbell at Stella's never stopped. People arrived at the house laden with sandwiches, lasagnes, curries and cakes. Neighbours pressed plates into everyone's hands and nearly spoon-fed the family. On the morning of the funeral, people came from everywhere. Buses pulled up outside from Sheriff Street, from Artane, from all parts of the city. We walked down Whitestown Drive, this mass of mourners and celebrants of Noel's life, and all the traffic stopped. It was such a sad time, but it was also such a magical time because it was a real celebration of humanity and community and Noel.

During those two days in Dublin, I also rekindled relationships with people I hadn't seen since I'd moved to London. And they all asked the same thing: 'Jesus, Jade, when are you coming home?'

'Never,' I said.

Yet, the funeral planted a question in my head: *What would moving back to Dublin be like?* I looked around me in awe at what was happening. *This would never happen in London,* I thought. *This incredible sense of warmth, love, neighbourhood and community doesn't exist there.* Noel's funeral was a really special event, and it marked another watershed moment in my life. I think it was the first time I started thinking, *What's really there for me in London?*

In another of those weird coincidences, my friends started to think the same way over the following year. We had all left Dublin and moved to London *for life*, and then something changed. It started one night when we were chatting in a bar, and someone – I'm not sure who – said, 'You know, girls, I'm thinking of going home.' And someone else responded, 'Well, actually, so am I.' And then we were all in the midst of this conversation, all admitting the same thing. Everyone was having second thoughts about living in London. And just like that, in the space of a single year, all of us came home.

It made perfect sense to return to Dublin because I was getting called to more and more auditions here. Tom didn't need much time to think about it either. He decided to look upon a move to Ireland as an opportunity for him too. We didn't hang around. We handed in our notice, and we moved to Dublin weeks later on a sunny day in July 2018, the day of my ma's birthday.

I still wasn't *sure* about moving back to Ireland. *This move doesn't have to be permanent*, I thought. *I'll give it a bash, but I can always move back to London if it doesn't work out.* I'd never thought that I would move back to my hometown, to be honest. I loved Ireland and the people, but I always expected London to be a better fit for me in the performing arts world.

I loved living in London for nine years and had the wildest of times, but the city is also a rat race, where everyone is constantly on the go. Everyone's mind is running at a hundred miles an hour. The girls reminded me recently how we actually used to take out diaries and schedule appointments with one another for coffee, or we'd never meet up. How mad is that? Even when I met friends, it was a frantic affair. My eyes would be rolling in my head, thinking of everything else I had to do that day.

The best thing about London is that everything is available on your doorstep. But it was dawning on me that, even though the choices were vast, I hadn't the income to enjoy a lot of them. My friends all had careers, secure jobs with good salaries and rising standards of living. I was starting out as an actor and never knew my income from week to week. Many people I knew had the money to go out several nights a week and enjoy everything the city had to offer. I didn't have that luxury.

I guess it's true what they say: everything changes once you change. Almost as soon as I got back, I started to get work. The relaxed and more casual environment of Dublin worked for me. There was more of a village atmosphere. Walking into an audition room in Dublin was always a bit of craic because people were happy to see you and dying to talk.

And everyone knows everyone in Dublin. I attended a costume fitting a few weeks ago, and I was worried because

I didn't know anyone else who was going. Then one person said, 'Oh, you worked on that, did you? You must know so-and-so ...' Immediately, I had a shared reference, someone in common. In the space of minutes, I got to know everyone. Irish people are welcoming anyway, so everything is more laidback. Auditions are like having a chat with friends now. The nerves never go, but I feel a lot more chilled at auditions once I do the graft in advance.

I've learned there's no magic to success in acting. Casting agents and directors want people who are easy to work with, people who are relaxed. Acting is all about timing too. Maybe it wasn't my time when I was younger. They talk about 'castability' in my business, and maybe I'm the right age. The stars seem to be aligning because I seem to be matching what casting agents are looking for. Sometimes, it's all about timing.

The changes in my life continued. 'You should try teaching drama!' my ma suggested. 'You love kids, and you're good with them. It would be perfect for you.' I've always worked with children. For eighteen months in London, one of my jobs was working in a school for children with special needs. But at first, I thought, *Oh God, no!* I didn't have the confidence to open my own business.

But Ma was determined that I at least give it a go, and she knew someone who had available space in a health centre. It all happened so fast that I hadn't time to think about it.

Within a week, I held an open day and signed up my first students. Then I approached two community centres in the local area and began teaching children with special needs one-on-one. Before I knew what was happening, I had opened a drama school for children, and I was running my own business.

I was the director, principal and teacher in a performing arts school called Jade Jordan's Westend Academy, teaching eighty-eight kids a week. I had so many children that I hired three other actors as teachers. I couldn't believe I was doing it. I could never have done that in the UK.

Working with kids is another of those connections with my nanny and ma. Nanny spent most of her life working with children. My ma does amazing work with children with special needs. She won't talk about it, but she is so caring when it comes to her job. I've seen her at work and seen how the children adore her. To me, she's like a little Mother Teresa, someone who massively underestimates herself and her contribution to the world. I knew that acting was what I always wanted to do, but like Nanny and Ma, I'm still drawn to working with children. Having my own performing arts school allows me to fulfil that need.

I also found a new sense of freedom when I started learning to drive for the first time in Dublin. The truth is, my world seemed to blossom as soon as I returned. Moving back turned out to be the best decision I ever made.

There were so many positives. Pariss was only twelve years old when I moved to London, so I missed all those years of my sister growing up. I always wanted a close relationship with Pariss, and for the first time, I began building a real adult connection with her. We're both at that age where we've clicked. We're best friends now, and I would have missed all that if I'd stayed in England.

My friends and soul sisters Fiona and Ciara came back from London around the same time as me. 'The Vengabus is comin', and everybody's on it,' they used to sing. And I just walk into their house and make myself at home. Their parents, Marian and Liamo, have made me feel like part of the family since I was going to primary school with Fiona. The couple get a great buzz from being around their kids and their friends. For me, being with the Heffernans is like my ma's relationship with Laura and Noel and Stella. There's another coincidence down the generations, and I didn't even think of that before I started working on this book. Fiona and Ciara and Marian and Liamo are like my extended family. Every show I do, they're front row on the first night. A piece about me appeared in one of the papers recently, and Liamo would have had it pinned up on the wall if he was allowed! He did the catering for my short film, and he'll be beside himself when he sees his name in the credits. I would have missed having these people back in my life if I stayed in London.

Tom did well in Ireland too. He landed a great job running a large store near Dundrum Shopping Centre almost immediately after arriving in Dublin. After all the years of struggle in London, I found myself living a wonderful life in my hometown. The truth is that I hadn't lived in Dublin for years, so Tom and I were like two tourists exploring the city every weekend. It seemed like things couldn't get any better, and then my agent called again.

'Are you sitting down?' she said. I wasn't, and my legs nearly went from under me when she told me I'd got a part in a new play to open in the Abbey Theatre. Can you imagine? It was my first role back in Ireland, and it was the Abbey! It's a massive dream for any actor to appear on the stage of the national theatre. The play, *Citysong* by Dylan Coburn Gray, is a story told across the generations and involves six actors playing sixty characters. The play would run in the Abbey for three weeks before moving to the West End in London for a month. The curtain was to come down on the show at the Galway Arts Festival. And Galway Arts Festival, as anyone knows, is all about craic. As gigs go, this was absolutely deadly.

Not everything can be rosy in the garden, though, can it? And as my professional life soared, my personal life started to go into a decline. Behind the scenes, Tom and I began to realise that we wanted different things. He didn't like living in Dublin. He hated it, in fact, and he wasn't settling. He's from the heart of London, and for him, Dublin was like a rural backwater.

We never fought. Ever. In all the years, we never argued over anything. There might have been the odd bicker over something silly like the ironing, and that was it. But things were changing between us; I could feel it.

Tom moved back to London just as the show in the Abbey opened, which was really bad timing. He left a mere ten months after we moved to Dublin. I knew Tom had grown up on London's busy streets, but I thought he didn't give my hometown enough time. I still don't think you can get to know any city in a few months.

In hindsight, I wouldn't want somebody to be unhappy because of me, but it wasn't how I felt at the time. We had been together for so long that it seemed like I was losing my right hand. I was very upset. Tom admitted later that he had regrets about his decision as soon as he got off the plane in London. But he had quit his job and said all his goodbyes by then. There was no going back.

Tom's return to London was not the end of our relationship. We had resolved to remain a couple, except now we were a couple living in two different countries. We were still a hundred per cent committed to each other. And then everything changed. A few months later, we attended a mutual friend's wedding in Suffolk, and it was so apparent that we were on different paths that we sat down the next day and had 'the conversation'. There wasn't any disagreement: it was time to call it a day. I had never thought it would happen to us, but I realised we had grown apart. My family were devastated when we broke up because they loved Tom and thought we'd be together forever. I miss his family too. They welcomed me into their hearts and were very good to me when I lived in London.

I'll always love Tom, but I had to accept that, somehow, we had changed and were on diverging roads. The only positive is that both of us came to that decision, and we remained friends, which helped make the break-up process easier. I'm proud that we have emerged from a relationship after that length of time and can still be friends. And I really do mean it when I say that I wish Tom all the love and happiness in the world.

I have no regrets about returning to Dublin. Everything has fallen into place for me since I came back. As much as I miss London, I don't plan to live there unless work brings me back. There is plenty in Dublin to keep me occupied. Even when Covid-19 restrictions meant that I had to close my drama school, I was kept busy filming.

It has only been through learning more about my nanny's and my ma's stories that I've fully realised for the first time how much we have in common. As I've said, we all went to England as young women, and against the odds, all three of us returned to live in Ireland. It seems like we all needed to go away before we really appreciated what we'd left behind. My nanny is beside herself about me living in Ireland again. Every time I get a new job, and it's happening far more often now, she says, 'Now, there you go, didn't I tell you? Best thing you ever did was come home.' And if history repeats itself – it certainly seems to in our family – it looks likely that Ireland will remain my home forever now, and I have to say I'm perfectly happy with that.

THERAPY

You'll probably think I'm mad when I tell you that I talked to dead people one night. To be fair, my yoga teacher would describe it differently. She'd say it was a guided visualisation to connect with the male side of my ancestry. I still say it's talking with dead people.

When I got back to Dublin, I started looking after myself more. I realised I'd shelved my own wellbeing for years, and I was no longer a kid in my twenties who could burn the candle at both ends.

I look at my nanny and ma, and they are grafters. They have been incredibly hard-working all their lives, and I aspire to be like them. In many ways, I know I'm like them. I never sit still, and I'm always tackling a million jobs at a time. I need to be busy.

At the moment, I'm writing this book, but I'm watching the clock because I have several self-tapes to do. A self-tape is a pre-recorded video audition where I read from a script in character. It's usually done with a friend who feeds the other character's dialogue to me.

When I go into the rehearsal process for a show, I'm with

the director or the writer, and I can rip through the script. I know where each character is coming from, where they've been, what they're about and what they want to achieve within the scene. I know so much about the character.

But for a self-tape or online audition, actors are left filling in the blanks. Often, I'd only get a page or a scene or two because there are all sorts of confidentiality issues involved. The only information I might get is that 'the character has grown up on a council estate, single mother, age twenty-five', and I'd be lucky to get that much detail. So I read the dialogue that I receive, and I make decisions about how to play my lines. Like I said, it's about filling in the blanks.

Then I edit the tapes, send them to my agent, and she submits them to casting directors. The hope is that I get called to the next stage in the audition process. I'm lucky because I get asked to do two or three self-tapes every week now. But it's also very time-consuming. It can take three hours to put a self-tape together properly, and obviously, you don't get paid for those audition hours every week. Most times, you send them off, and you never hear anything back. It's all unpaid work, but it has to be done to bag the next gig.

If I'm lucky enough to get the job and the writing is good, the lines inform me, and it's easy to get into the headspace of my character. I keep reading the lines, keep reading the script, and try to be truthful to it.

I'm not a method actor – in the sense that I need to embody

the character, and nobody's allowed to talk to me because I'm 'in the zone' – for me, it's simpler. Once I stay truthful to the lines, the character just comes. I did a self-tape with the help of a friend recently, about a mother who discovers her husband was abusing their child. I don't have a child or a husband, so how would I know exactly how that feels? But when I say the lines, and I'm truthful to them, the emotion comes. I never find it hard to cry because I'm a crier anyway. But the more emotional a scene, the more it takes out of me. I haven't had the luxury of delving into a character and eating, breathing, sleeping and living her for a few weeks. I'm not at the point yet, but I know I will get there. I will get to that lead role eventually.

Apart from shooting self-tapes, I'm always learning lines for whatever job I have coming up. Anyone who doesn't do acting thinks that learning the lines must be the hardest part of the job. But I don't find it hard at all. It's all muscle memory. I just read and read and read the lines until they're in my head. But I've learned that you can lose that muscle memory very fast. The first self-tape I recorded after we came back from the first Covid-19 lockdown had only about four lines, and I just couldn't learn them. The words wouldn't sink in because I'd been out of practice for two or three months. Now that I'm back in practice again, I can learn an entire scene in fifteen minutes. The brain is a phenomenal thing because it can retain so much.

Actors do forget lines – we're only human, and theatre is live and very raw. Doing theatre is very rewarding, but it's nerve-wracking before you go on. I call them the NWs or the nervous wees. You keep thinking you need to go to the toilet, but you don't. It's all nerves. I'm just petrified, and I'm having palpitations – it actually feels like my heart is bursting out of my chest. And don't get me started on the sweating. That adrenalin shock fades away at some point on the stage, and I find myself loving it or being so immersed in it that I don't even remember doing it afterwards. That's where you want to be as an actor because when that happens, and you lose yourself in the role, it's magical.

Thankfully, it's never happened where I've gone completely blank or messed up my cue or lines on stage. I'm sure it will happen, but the thing is that we're a team, an ensemble. The other actors might know if you've fluffed your lines, but the audience rarely will. The actors are there to step in and support each other on stage. Of course, working in film and TV is much more forgiving, but you don't want to be fluffing your lines there either because the crew will end up hating you if they have to keep doing take after take!

Recording self-tapes and learning lines are just part of the professional acting process. There's always so much going on. In early 2021 days, I was down in Galway working with Druid Theatre. I was also shooting a cool film documentary on HIV. I have a series called *Kin* coming out in September

2021 on AMC and RTÉ, and I'm shooting for a series called *Redemption*, which will be screened on Virgin Media and ITV in 2022. Work brings me abroad sometimes, which is really great, and I'm flying to Eastern Europe soon for a shoot. In the meantime, I'm always trying to improve my craft by attending workshops. I'm also staying in touch with the community centres and planning to reopen my performing arts school after Covid restrictions are fully lifted.

It's hectic, and I need to be healthy to stay on top of everything. As soon as I got back to Dublin and found a bit of job stability for the first time, I began to invest in a healthier lifestyle. Everyone is more aware of the link between physical and mental health these days and the importance of self-care. I have to admit, I never consciously thought about Nanny's mental health issues when I made changes to my life. I kind of forgot those years of her being in Saint Patrick's until I started writing this book. It's easy to forget because she came out the other side of her illness, and as a child, I was never really aware of anything apart from those two indentations on her head.

My move towards a healthier lifestyle was really influenced by my hippy-chick friends here. 'You can't keep going on like you are,' they said. 'You need to look after yourself better.' The self-care journey began slowly. I started going to the gym and learning to train. Two of my friends are yoga teachers, so I was also drawn into yoga and gong meditation or sound escape. I'm not claiming to be a guru, and I don't meditate all the time, but when I feel like my body's calling me to slow down, I try to. I love spending time in the outdoors now too. I've learned that being in nature soothes body, mind and soul.

I'm so glad I made that conscious decision to look after myself better when I did. Writing this book has reminded me how Nanny looked after everyone except herself. She let things go with her health, and she's losing her eyesight as a result. I think of my ma and all the running around she did for us, and how her health is affected too. She's not well a lot of the time. I could have ended up in ill-health too, and it's not to say that I still won't, but I'm giving myself a fighting chance. My nanny and ma didn't have that opportunity. They didn't have half an hour to themselves to light a stick of incense, lie down on a yoga mat and put their hands together. And they would have been regarded as mad yokes if they did.

My ma thinks I'm a bit mad as it is. I do boxing and train four times a week, and she sometimes says that I do too much. But I only have one tool for my work, and my tool is my body. I have no choice but to look after it. I have to be ready for whatever physical and mental demands the job requires of me.

My yoga teacher, Kitty Maguire, came into my life when I really needed her. She had a massively positive impact on me. She practices Shakti or womb yoga, which works on healing.

Her classes, which use visualisation techniques, were always really fascinating.

I never had a connection with our family's male side apart from Ma's brothers. I have a great relationship with my uncles James and Jason. Maybe it's because I was their first niece and the first of a new generation that I'm so close to them both, but they're the only ones on the male side I know. So, to be honest, I didn't expect much as Kitty led us to a peaceful, dimly lit room in our minds one evening and urged us to seek ancestors who were willing to work with us and guide us on our path. She assured us any ancestors who wanted to provide help would reach out to us.

For a long time, I lay there and visualised nothing. I felt relaxed and serene lying on my yoga mat, but nothing was happening. So I remained in this room in my mind and had given up on meeting my ancestors when – I'm not kidding you – a man appeared out of nowhere.

He was Black-skinned, tall, with tightly cropped hair, and had a warm and welcoming face. I immediately liked him, but I didn't know who he was. I don't even recall an accent, but I remember his words. 'You're doing great work. Keep going with what you're doing. Don't worry – you're on the right track.'

I had so many questions to ask, but Kitty started to pull us out of our meditation, and he faded away. My immediate response was a sense of frustration. It had taken so long for me to visualise anything, but he was gone before I had time to learn more. When we spoke as a group about our experiences afterwards, that's when the tears came. I didn't expect it, but the whole experience really moved me. The space that Kitty manages to create is full of positive healing messages for the mind and body. I needed that safe and supportive space at the time.

I'm fortunate to have so many friends who are into self-improvement and self-help and who are all hippies at heart. Nowadays, I'm always looking to make myself stronger and to be the best version of myself. One of my yoga friends suggested the benefits of working with another wellness professional, and she introduced me to Karen Dwyer, who works as a neuro-coach. Similar to a life coach, she uses scientific tools from neuroscience and psychology to help clients.

I worked with Karen for nearly four months, and I talked about issues that I had never raised before in my life. I spoke about being an individual again after being part of a couple for so many years. I'd met Tom when I was young, so it was like I was always part of a team. I love being on my own, and I've always loved my own company, but it's still an adjustment being single after being in a relationship for so long.

While writing this story, I'm also struck by the fact that my nanny ended up on her own, and my mother has been on her own for a long time. Ma is genuinely single by choice and happy with that. I know another family friend, a woman who has been on her own for twenty years and is adamant that she doesn't want another relationship. 'Never again!' she says. 'I'm not interested.' So I know being single works for some people. And I'm happy being on my own at the moment. But sometimes, when I have a bad day, it would be nice to have someone to hold and cuddle me and tell me it'll all be grand.

To be honest, I've looked at those apps where you swipe to the left or right, but they're not for me. I'm old school. I prefer to leave it to fate and bump into somebody on a train or in a coffee shop. For now, things are great, but eventually, I know I want to share my life with a partner. Nanny and Ma are happy with their lives, but I've realised I don't want to be single for the rest of my life. No way. I'm just not in any great rush to find someone right now.

Of course, there were plenty of other issues to discuss with Karen apart from being newly single. And I found it worthwhile talking with someone who's objective; someone who sees everything from the perspective of an outsider.

I'll share one weird experience with you, one that taught me the subconscious is an amazing thing. When I was working in the Abbey Theatre, I walked past a particular bus stop every day, and I felt this strange, almost overwhelming wave of emotion.

It's hard to explain, but this came over me every day as I passed the bus stop. I couldn't figure out what was going on. The feeling was very intense, yet I couldn't identify it. It wasn't fear. I just felt a heightened response to being there, but I couldn't put my finger on the emotion. All I knew was that it made me feel uncomfortable. I tried to explain the sensations I experienced, and Karen attempted to draw me out about it.

'Why that bus stop?'

'It's the one to Blanchardstown.'

'So it's a stop that you use all the time?'

'No, not since I was a kid. We've had a car for years, and then I was in London, and I'm driving now.'

'The last time you used that bus stop, what age would you have been?'

'I don't know. It's a long time ago now.'

'Did you take the bus on your own?'

'No, I would have been too young then, I suppose.'

'So who would have been there with you?'

'My ma, I suppose … or my da.'

She drew me out on the subject of my father for a while. 'You've so much hurt inside you because of him,' I remember her saying.

I shook my head. 'I don't. Really, I don't,' I said. 'I never think of him.'

When it came to my father, I always believed that I couldn't miss what I'd never had. I always said that I wasn't affected by the lack of a father figure in my life.

'I turned out fine without him, didn't I?' I said.

It was only through explorations with Karen that I realised the emotions stirred by this bus stop were rooted back in my da. I started having memories of my father and me taking the bus home from town. I may have blocked these memories out for years and not realised it.

I've been really lucky because I had a fantastic mother who provided everything, all the physical and emotional support I needed in life. She did all the work that two people normally do. She was incredible when you think of it. Working full-time, raising two of us, and all the fun we used to have too. Ma always made sure we went on holidays abroad every year. We were spoilt.

Sure, there were times when I'd look at other teenagers with their mas and das. I was a bit wistful at times. I thought it would be nice to have a da as well. But most of the time, I didn't think about it. I had one parent doing the work of two and doing a perfectly good job of it. My ma was my rock, and she's always been the core of our strong family unit.

It was Karen who insisted I was carrying hurt from that relationship or lack of it. I shrugged those notions off at first. I'd grown up regarding my father as an irrelevant figure, this shadowy figure from my distant past. I thought his absence never affected me, but subconsciously it must have been on my mind. How else can I explain the emotional impact of walking past that bus stop? The subconscious is an amazing thing. It holds on to so many things that you're unaware of.

If my father ever crosses my mind now, it's to wonder how some people can bring children into the world and then leave them. I find that so strange. I imagine I would do anything for my children. I have eighty-eight of them in my drama school, and I cherish all of them. And they're not even my family! I can't understand a person who cuts off all contact with their children and never sees them growing up. It was his choice not to be a part of my life. But I've always felt that life is too short to concern myself with people who don't care about me. I prefer to concern myself with people who cherish me and care about me and who want me in their lives – my family, extended family and friends.

All these types of therapy and self-care have made me appreciate the importance of looking after myself. In the past, I always put other people's welfare before my own and sometimes left myself burnt out. I was forever getting minor ailments like colds, tonsillitis and ear infections. Now I can't remember the last time I was sick. Once I slowed down and took care of myself, I found myself feeling stronger, and capable of caring more effectively for everybody else.

One of the most useful things Karen taught me was to journal and document how I felt. She urged me to write forgiveness letters to people who hurt me. Forgiveness letters are a bloody fantastic idea. I never thought writing a letter could be such an effective therapy, but it is cathartic to sit down and pour out your heart and soul on paper. The best part is that you never have to send these letters.

I wrote forgiveness letters to some people, apology letters to others, but they were about *my* feelings, no one else's, so I just ripped them up afterwards. And it worked. So many things were resolved. I could walk past that bus stop without a wave of emotion threatening to overwhelm me.

It's only through exploring Nanny's and Ma's pasts for this book that I've considered yet another weird coincidence – that we all lost our fathers in various ways early in life. I don't believe that growing up without a dad shaped me in any negative way. I know Nanny, Ma and me have always been very self-sufficient and independent. Did we end up more driven and more determined to prove ourselves because we had no father figures in our lives? To be honest, I think that's giving too much credit to absent fathers.

Yes, we're three generations of hard-working and driven women, but that's probably because we were born that way.

BLACK IRISH HISTORY

All my life, I've had difficulty persuading people that I'm Irish, born and reared, and so have my ma and sister. The funny thing is that Ireland has a long multiracial history, stretching back hundreds of years. The first mention of a Black person in Ireland was in the 1500s, and up to ten thousand Black or mixed-race people lived in Ireland by the nineteenth century.

There's also a strong history of Black and mixed-race people who have made their living in showbusiness like me. Phil Lynott is one of the most famous Black Irish stars of recent times, but it was a Black Irish woman who was one of the biggest pop stars in Ireland and England in the eighteenth century. Rachael Baptist was a singing sensation who performed regularly in theatres, music halls and events after making her debut in Dublin in February 1750.

Nothing is known of her early life except that she was born in Ireland. She married a music teacher called John Crow and began appearing under her married name, Rachael Crow, regularly performing in venues and at great events across England and Ireland. According to the records, she sang in

Belfast on 30 August 1773, and her fate after that remains a mystery.

The circus was arriving as a new entertainment form just as Rachael Baptist disappeared. By the 1820s, a Black Irish acrobat called Pablo Paddington became one of the great circus stars of the era. Ryan's Olympic Circus posters describe him as 'the celebrated Man of Colour on the flying rope!' He was also known 'the Flying African', performing with famous English circus companies such as Astley's. Pablo was actually born and raised in Cork by an Irish father and a mother from Haiti.

His brother, George John Paddington, joined the priesthood, and newspapers reported he was the first Black person in the world to receive a doctorate at a European university after he studied theology in Germany.

Ireland's long struggle for freedom from Great Britain meant that many people sympathised with Black slaves and the abolitionists in America. Maybe that's why there seemed to be very little racism in Ireland back then. The *Belfast News-Letter* described racism as 'sordid and contemptible' in 1786, and Black abolitionists were treated like celebrities when they brought their anti-slavery campaigns to Ireland.

Black author Olaudah Equiano toured all over the country for eight months in 1791–2, when the global slave trade was thriving. Born in Africa, he and his sister were enslaved as children and shipped to Virginia in America. He was sold to a ship's captain and never saw his sister again. Encouraged by an Irish sailor, he learned to read and write at sea and bought his own freedom when he was twenty years old. He was treated like a rock star when he came to Ireland promoting abolition.

American abolitionist and writer Frederick Douglass spent four months in Ireland. When he was leaving in January 1846, his words tell a wonderful story: 'I can truly say, I have spent some of the happiest moments of my life since landing in this country.'

The story about the Black Irish island, Montserrat, in the Caribbean is an amazing one too. Back in Cromwellian times, hundreds of people from Ireland, many of them from Cork, were transported to Montserrat in the West Indies as political prisoners. They arrived in the 1600s around the same time as the first African slaves. The Irish and the Africans had a lot in common, so they lived together peacefully, and many of them integrated.

The legacy of the Irish remains all over the Caribbean island today. You can still hear the lilt of the Cork accent in the dark-skinned population. Kinsale is one of the main towns on the island, and passports are stamped with a shamrock. The island is home to a unique race of Black Irish people who celebrate St Patrick's Day as a big national holiday. How great is that?

I never knew until recently about the diverse Black Irish community that existed in Ireland for hundreds of years. Or about that Black Irish island in the Caribbean. It all goes to show that there is a far greater shared history between Black and Irish than many of us ever imagined.

SILENCE

Just a couple of weeks ago, I had to drop off a friend's phone charger at the Abbey Theatre where he was working. It was rush hour, a busy evening and this middle-aged man and I realised we were on a collision course on the pavement. We did that dance that people do: I went left, and he went left at the same time, and then we both went right at the same time.

'Sorry!' I said.

'You stupid fucking n***er,' he said.

We both walked on. It took a few seconds for the man's words to sink in. *Did he really just say that? Did he call me the n-word?* I swerved around, and there he was, metres away from me, standing at a Luas stop. This man was in his fifties, wearing jeans and a jacket. He was like any ordinary man, probably on his way home to his family from work. He wasn't carrying cans of beer; he wasn't dishevelled. He didn't appear to be under the influence of drink or drugs.

I stormed over to him. 'How dare you speak to me like that,' I said. 'Don't you dare speak to anyone like that!'

His eyes widened. 'Whoa, I wasn't expecting that!' he said.

I wasn't expecting that! I don't know what he expected. Did he not expect to be confronted? Did he not expect me to speak English? I don't know. I stood glaring at him, and other people standing at the Luas stop watched me, wondering about this crazy woman who was apparently accosting a stranger for no reason. There was no apology from him. He glanced to the sky and then started studying his shoes as if I wasn't there at all. I couldn't think of anything else to say, so I stormed off again.

What else could I do? I wasn't expecting that either. *You stupid fucking n***er?* I was livid and really upset. I haven't been called the n-word in a long time, and all the feelings of hurt and humiliation flooded back in an instant. I felt vulnerable to attack again. I couldn't believe a grown man had spoken to me like that, yet I'm pretty sure it won't be the last time I'll hear it. A friend managed to put it in perspective for me later.

'You told him how you felt. You didn't let him get away with it, and God knows what's going on in that sad man's life that he needs to speak to somebody like that,' she said.

And I know she's right. It doesn't pardon his behaviour, but I have to accept that whatever is going on in his life it can't be good. That's a healthier way of looking at these things rather than getting angry about it. It's difficult sometimes, but I need to feel sympathy for these people who have so much hatred in their souls.

Even as I write about this incident, I'm reminded of my ma telling me the story of something similar happening to her more than forty years ago. My ma was a schoolgirl then. Isn't it mad that this is *still* happening to people on the streets of Dublin?

Racism should be a rare phenomenon now that people of colour are much more visual and prominent in Irish society. Who would have thought a few years ago that an openly gay, mixed-race man could become the leader of this country? Everyone has their own opinions about Leo Varadkar, but it's fair to say he broke the mould in Irish politics when he was Taoiseach.

There's a presumption that each new generation becomes more tolerant and open-minded than its predecessor. I'm not sure that's happened in America, but Ireland seems to be making progress. Unfortunately, you'll always bump into the occasional dope on the street, and you'll find plenty more of them on social media.

Sometimes, too, I feel like banging my head off a wall when I meet people who won't accept that I'm as Irish as they are. A while ago, I sat outside a café in Portobello, Dublin, with a friend who is Irish but lives in London. He's a mixed-race guy whose father is from Sri Lanka. A stranger ambled along the street and then made a beeline for us.

'Do youse have a smoke?'

'Sorry,' my friend said. 'We don't smoke.'

He looked us both up and down. 'Where are youse from anyway?'

'Dublin,' my friend replied.

The man gave us this look that said, 'Yeah, youse are, all right,' and he went on his way.

We turned to each other and laughed. What else can you do? Why is it still so hard to believe that Irish people come in all colours these days?

My sister is much paler skinned than me. She can look darker in the summer, but mostly she looks light skinned. Even so, people can detect an ethnic difference, so she receives offensive comments too.

'Go back to China – you don't belong here!' some muppets told her recently. China? I don't know where they get that from, but this mindlessness pisses me off sometimes.

My two pet hates are the terms 'n***er' and 'Paki' because they are the two terms of abuse I've heard throughout my life. The term 'Paki' probably grates on me the most. People don't even understand what they're saying when they call me that. They're calling me a Pakistani even though I have no connection to that part of the world at all. None of my family has been there in their lives either. And what's wrong with being from Pakistan anyway? Yet it's hurled as a form of abuse from people who don't even understand what they're saying.

People can experience more passive-aggressive or sly forms of racism too. My mother, her brother and Pariss went into a bar for lunch a while ago. The three sat there waiting for service for a while, and a couple arrived and sat at the table next to them. Within minutes, the couple got menus, and their orders were taken, but no one served my ma's table.

My uncle went up to the bar and asked, 'Can we order, please?' The barman said: 'Someone will be down to take your order straight away.' Five minutes later, my uncle asked a passing lounge girl, who assured them their order would be taken in a minute. Ten minutes later, my mother went up to the bar, and she was told the same thing. 'Someone will be down to take your order straight away,' the barman said.

The couple who'd come in after them received their food, and my mother realised this wasn't just bad service. Something more was going on.

'Is there a problem?' she asked the barman. 'We've been sitting here ages, and nobody has taken our order.'

'No, there's no problem,' he said.

This time the couple on the next table intervened. 'There must be some problem,' the woman said. 'These people were here before us, and we've been served our food, and no one has even taken their order. They've asked several times. Why aren't you taking their order?'

The barman replied with the same mantra. 'Someone will be down to take your order straight away.'

And still, other people's orders were taken, and the barman continued to ignore my ma's table. They didn't imagine that they were deliberately ignored. The people at the next table saw it and were appalled by it too. The couple tried to insist they were served, but my mother, sister and uncle, all decent, hard-working people, had enough public humiliation. They left without being served. Can you imagine that? That's not a nice thing for any human being to experience.

The truth is that random abuse from strangers is a significant source of stress and trauma for people of colour. We never know when it is going to happen. I know I could be walking down the street, or I could be in a supermarket, and someone could turn on me. It's distressing when it does happen. It can leave me feeling vulnerable, isolated and humiliated. I've often walked away and cried my eyes out afterwards. I'll never do it in front of these people – I won't give them that satisfaction – but it does hurt.

It goes on every day in Ireland, and other people are subjected to this kind of abuse far more than I am. And it's a very small minority of eejits that behaves this way. So what can we do about it? This kind of thing rarely takes place behind closed doors. The abuse is usually in public and within sight and earshot of others. Yet people often stand back and do nothing.

We should speak up if we hear someone being racist, we can pull them up on it. We all have a little racism and sexism in us to some degree. Nobody's perfect, but we can do better. Sometimes, it's as simple as saying 'It's not OK to say that' or 'Please don't talk to people like that.' If our elderly uncle or our younger brother says something cruel or racist, we need to challenge them.

For the sake of the next generation of children, we need to change things. We can choose to be activists and help make a better world, or we can do nothing and support the muppets out there. Let's choose action over inaction. Most of us don't plan to hurt other people intentionally, but we can sometimes do it through complacency.

SKIN DEEP

Looking back over everything I've learned, I realise Nanny remains an enigma. I'm not sure, even after spending hours and hours talking to her about her life, I fully understand what went on a lot of the time. I'm so close to her, yet she keeps a lot to herself. Nanny is always 'fine', even if she's not. She will never tell you when she's suffering, and she will do anything to avoid confrontation. She's a sensitive soul and a bright, loving and intelligent woman, but she keeps so much to herself. She refuses to be a worry or a burden to anyone.

My nanny claims that she 'never saw colour', and some people believe that's a derogatory thing to say these days. They claim that saying 'I don't see colour' is like saying 'I am denying your racial identity because it makes me more comfortable'. I can't speak for anybody else, but in my nanny's case, I really believe she doesn't see colour. Anyone can pop up in front of Nanny painted purple with green spots, and she won't blink. She won't notice. Anyone who knows her knows that. At the same time, she has admitted that she used to feel self-conscious when people stared at Larry in Ireland. She must have noticed that other people saw colour.

She also says there was no prejudice against her interracial marriage in London, and the only discrimination she experienced was in Ireland. I find that hard to believe. From what I've read, racism would have been an everyday experience for immigrants and interracial couples in Britain in the sixties and seventies. It's difficult to see how she lived in London with a Black husband and mixed-race children without encountering racist abuse.

The year after Nanny married our Black grandfather, Conservative candidate Peter Griffiths won a seat in the UK general election using the slogan 'If you want a n***er for a neighbour, vote Liberal or Labour'. Can you imagine? Clearly, institutional and casual racism are still prevalent in the UK today. People can still recall the signs 'No Blacks, no Irish, no dogs' in London right into the sixties. I'm sure Nanny would have been doubly shunned being Irish with a Black husband.

Was Nanny lucky that she managed to avoid prejudice and discrimination? I don't think she could have been. But her way of dealing with things is to erase negative experiences from her mind. I don't know why she remembers the negative in Ireland, but maybe she recalls it because it was more personal to her. It was home. It was family. Mostly, she prefers to see the better side of people and remember the positive. Nanny 'forgets' things that she doesn't want to remember. There are so many questions I have about events in her life, but she has no answers.

I wonder why Nanny took her three children, left a comfortable home in London and returned to Ireland with no job, no support and no roof over her head. That remains a mystery to us all. Nanny will only say it was something she felt she had to do. Whatever the reason, it triggered the end of her marriage to my grandfather, Larry Coleman.

The fascinating thing is that Nanny wrote to her husband thirty years or so after they lost contact. She told us that she had a dream about Larry and felt compelled to write to him. In 2011, she posted the letter to the last known address she had for him, a house about six miles from Walthamstow. She received a note by return from a woman who thanked her for her lovely letter but regretted informing Nanny that Larry had died from cancer twelve years earlier. The woman referred to Larry as her father, so it's clear that my grandfather had another family or at least another daughter.

At that time, I was living in London, and I was itching to find out more. I even considered turning up on their doorstep but managed to resist the temptation. It's not clear from the return letter if Larry's daughter was aware of her father's relationship with Nanny. In fact, the reply to Nanny's letter left more questions than it answered. I still don't have the answers to those questions, and my sister and I are the only ones who want to know more. We're the nosy ones in the family because everyone else prefers to leave it in the past. I guess I can understand those feelings too.

If Nanny is an enigma, Ma is inscrutable. She is a very private person who prefers to keep things to herself. She's been through a lot in her life and had to be tough to survive. My mother is still a young woman, yet when she was growing up, performers were still blacking up their faces on a peak-time TV show on the BBC. The *Black and White Minstrel Show* was still considered prime-time family entertainment on a Saturday night when she left Britain at age twelve.

She grew up in Dublin in the late seventies, in the toughest of times and circumstances. She looked after her family and protected them when she was nothing but a child herself. Then she protected her daughters as a single mother when she became an adult. Her colour has greatly influenced her life. In one way, it has made her strong and self-reliant, and in another, it has made her wary and distrustful.

The roots of this book began when I lived in London. As an actor, work comes and goes, and there are downtimes. I have other skills and experience that allow me to work in retail, restaurant and bars, so I was always grafting and never really had downtimes. But I wanted to work in the performing arts, not as a waitress or in sales. There were times when I would get stressed, and I'd be hard on myself. *You're wasting your time trying to be an actor.* This is the first time in my life that I've actually been able to say 'I'm an actor', and I no longer subsidise my living by waitressing or selling or any of the multitude of jobs I used to do. But back then, working full-time as an actor was only a dream. And it's not great for your self-esteem to be waiting for the phone to ring.

I started thinking of ways to create acting opportunities for myself, including writing a script and shooting it. My friend David suggested, 'Why not use your own family history as the subject matter?' And I thought, *Why not?* As an actor, it would make sense to write my own material and bring this story to life.

I only knew the basic bones of my family's story when I started. I'd picked up things about my family's life as a kid, so I knew there was an interesting story there. But at the same time, I knew very little. I took out a video camera and started asking my grandmother questions about her life.

I didn't have many expectations at the start, apart from adding another skillset to my acting and learning more about my family history. But the more I dug into it, the more fascinated I became with the story. And the more I asked, the more I realised how little I knew. I also suspected there was a lot my nanny and my ma were not telling me. Ma has always said I should have been a detective. She says I was nosy from the beginning, and my neck was constantly extended from the pram, twisting this way and that to see what was going on. I always wanted to know more and more, and I still do.

I'm sure they've both allowed me only tiny glimpses into their lives, but much of what I learned shocked me. I knew things were hard in the past, but I didn't realise how hard. I didn't know how harsh life was for Nanny and Ma. The fact that my ma and her brothers were left on a wall outside their own grandmother's house still floors me. I have poked and prodded, but I still haven't got all the answers I hoped for.

At the same time, in the process of writing this, I discovered events and details that are still too raw and too private to share. There have also been occasions where I would like to reveal more, but to do so would have risked hurting people close to me. It's been a balancing act and a huge learning curve.

All the pent-up feelings I experienced while learning about my family's story found a voice in May of 2020 when I watched George Floyd suffocate under a police officer's knee. My heart hurt. It really did. I asked Ma and Nanny to do some more audios with me, and I posted excerpts of their experiences on Instagram. They were simple audios with their words rolling in white on a black screen. The response to those audios astonished me. People I have known for years had no idea what my family went through or what some people of colour still go through every day.

As protests erupted worldwide over George Floyd's death, writing this story and recording these audios felt like my protest, my small bit of resistance. George Floyd did nothing to justify the brutal actions that ended his life, and overwhelming evidence, including the traumatic video footage, convinced twelve jurors of that fact in April 2021. Derek Chauvin's guilty verdict was a watershed moment that may provide some healing and change.

There have been big changes in Ireland over the last few years, many positive ones where people of colour are concerned. Modern Ireland is a great place to live, but racist abuse still happens. Some people and ethnicities are experiencing unnecessary hardship. I realised by the reaction to my Instagram posts that many Irish people are not aware of that.

My family's story was the first thing that came to mind when Screen Ireland launched a competition for actors to produce and star in their own short films last year. I decided to pitch a story roughly based on events in their lives. The plot features an interracial couple, Annalise and Chris. I play Annalise, who is rejected by her racist father-in-law but has a loving relationship with her mother-in-law until the woman's sudden death. Annalise is devastated when Chris tells her that his dad doesn't want her at his mother's funeral. Pieces of my family history are blended with fiction in the screenplay.

You can't imagine how thrilled I was when my script was one of those chosen in the competition. I am now one of the first Black women to write, produce and star in a short film funded and supported by Screen Ireland. Seeing my work and hearing my own words on the screen is such an amazing feeling. It's electric to see it all come together. The dream has always been to do a feature film about my family's story, but a short film is a good start.

It also feels good to represent this new diverse Ireland in the world of film. Hopefully, I can inspire young children who look like me to believe that they too can follow their dreams.

Ireland has become a dramatically different place compared to a few years ago. I grew up with no role models, no one who looked like me outside of my immediate family. I didn't look like my teachers, my classmates, my neighbours, my friends. My dolls were blonde, and so were Disney princesses.

But that's all changed now. My young adult life is very different from Nanny's and Ma's. Instead of seeing actors in blackface on TV like my ma, I am working in the performing arts world. I watch Black people in soaps, and I see mixed-race people on TV. I shared the Abbey stage last year with a good friend who is also mixed-race. There are ethnic dolls and ethnic Disney princesses now. When I walk outside my door, I see many ethnicities and many skin colours. If I eat out at night, I can choose from a vast array of Irish, European and Asian restaurants. It's a different world from the country I grew up in.

We are a multicultural society in Ireland now, and we are surrounded by diversity. Many Irish people accept and celebrate our new world. But as the French say: 'plus ça change, plus c'est la même chose' or 'the more things change, the more they stay the same'. Because the hard truth is that some don't welcome this new diversity.

Colour is, as they say, only skin deep, yet many people still face shame, victimisation, marginalisation and other obstacles because their skin contains more melanin than others. How mad is that? My nanny went through this in Ireland more than fifty years ago. My mam went through this after her. And a middle-aged man felt he had a right to call me a 'stupid fucking n***er' on a busy Dublin street just recently. These kinds of experiences are soul-crushing. I don't want my kids or my sister's children or anyone's kids to encounter the mindless harassment of earlier generations.

We can all play our part by calling out casual racism when we hear it. Saying 'I'm not racist' is not enough. Saying nothing when someone says 'I am not a racist but ...' which is only a prelude to saying something completely racist, is not an option. Stating 'I am *anti-racist*' is the only way to commit to the beautiful resistance. We need to educate ourselves as best we can. We have to think about what we say and educate our kids and our grandkids. We need to educate the older generations, the aunts and uncles and grandparents who make the odd racist comment.

I've seen this cultural shift in our perceptions of sexual harassment in the workplace with the #MeToo movement.

A sexist worldview is being turned on its head because women are speaking out and saying 'We're not putting up with this crap anymore!' There is a lot more work to do to make a real impact in the workplace, but the #MeToo movement has helped us break the silence and demonstrate consequences for bad behaviour. Cultural change can come about miraculously fast when people put their minds to it.

And no skin colour is exempt from self-examination when it comes to racism. We all have to challenge pervasive stereotypes and bias. We can all contribute to creating a world where everybody is accepted and valued as a member of the community. Skin colour should never come into the equation and should never shape anyone's life.

For me, it would also be great to see an end to this unconscious bias where 'Black' equals 'other' and does not correlate with 'Irish'. I am tired of the words 'But where are you really from?' It's simple, and I don't think it's a lot to ask. I just want to be the proud Irish woman I am without my identity being constantly questioned. My ma and my sister do too.

Nanny's eighty-ninth birthday this year was our first real family gathering in ages. Normally, we all meet up in the Brock Inn, a family-run traditional pub in north county Dublin, for Nanny's birthdays. Nanny loves their corned beef or turkey and ham – hearty food, nothing fancy.

This year, we had to forgo that small treat because

everywhere was still in lockdown, and we told her we'd have a small birthday tea in Ma's house instead. For the first time in ages, she got dressed up and did her hair.

Then I noticed she was carrying a new purse. Nanny's not a hoarder, but she holds onto things far longer than she should. She's used to being frugal, I suppose. She never wastes things, and her old purse was as old as me. It was shabby and black and held together by layers of sticky tape.

'Janey, new purse, Nanny? Where's your old purse gone? It's not like you to throw anything out.'

She started rummaging in the bin she keeps by her chair and plucked the old purse out. She turned it this way and that in her hand, and she sighed. 'It looks like it has the mange, doesn't it?'

God, she made me laugh. And that's Nanny. She cracks me up with some of the things she comes out with. She utters these unexpected gems sometimes, and I love it. I love her and all her eccentricities. I see bits of Nanny in me, in that she's soft like I am. I can come across as really strong, but I'm not. I cry over anything, and I wear my heart on my sleeve. And I see bits of Ma in me too. I graft like she does, and I'm always *go, go, go* like she is. And looks-wise, everyone says I'm the image of my ma when she was my age. But personality-wise, I guess I'm placid and easy-going like my nanny.

Nanny didn't expect much for her birthday this year. It was only when we arrived at Ma's place that she realised all the family was there. I saw Pariss with her fiancé, Ross, and Stella with her daughter, Laura, and her granddaughter, Lucy. Uncle James was there with his son, Josh – everyone significant in Nanny's life was there. My cousin Donna and I laughed about the day we fed Uncle Joseph the cans of beer. God forgive us, but we've kept that quiet from Nanny all these years. We still haven't admitted doing that to this day.

Ma brought out cakes and sandwiches, and we all had a photo session with Nanny, everyone trying to get their own pictures with her. Whenever we were grumpy as kids, Nanny used to say 'Smile and give your face a holiday'. But she refuses to smile for photos. I don't know why, but she doesn't like to smile for the camera. So we were slagging her and yelling, 'Smile and give your face a holiday!' and trying to make her laugh.

I remember looking around as Ma brought out the birthday cake, and we all gathered around Nanny to sing 'Happy Birthday'. And I realised that Nanny is the one who brings us all together. Sometimes we don't see each other from one end of the year to the other, but everyone gathers for her. I can still see Nanny so clearly that night. Her eyes are shining, and she can't help beaming despite all the phone cameras pointed in her direction. And she looks great, the same old Nanny. She has always looked old, but she never seems to grow older, if you know what I mean. Her skin tone is so pale and translucent, it's alabaster in colour, and her hair is snowy white too. I can't help but marvel at how different we all look. I can still see Ma singing her heart out and my sister throwing her head back laughing. And once again, I feel that familiar wave of happiness and gratitude that I'm part of this wonderful family.

I love my family, and I'm proud of and grateful for what Nanny and Ma achieved despite the odds stacked against them. I'm proud of what Pariss and I have achieved. For an ordinary working-class Dublin family, we've had an extraordinary journey.

Maybe it's an age thing, but my confidence as a young Irish woman has finally come around. It seems this country has come of age too. We are far more confident as a society. Ireland has changed, continues to change and is a place where we have a greater diversity of ideas, nationalities, ethnicities, races, religions, food … everything. And the place is so much the better for it. It's a great country, and when we all learn to respect and cherish all these differences, it will be an even better country. There's an old saying: 'A lot of different flowers make a bouquet'. Aren't they wise and beautiful words?

It's only in the last few years that I've come to love who I am and feel comfortable in my own skin. It's the kind of confidence that comes with age, really. As teenagers, we're always too fat or too spotty. Regardless of colour, we go through that I-hate-everything-about-myself phase. I had hang-ups about myself in the way that I hated my hair and my compulsive showering. That gradually changed in my twenties as my confidence grew, and I began to embrace everything that made me unique instead of trying to fit in all the time. When I turned thirty, though, I really hit maturity, and my perspective and outlook on life changed completely. Everything slotted into place, and I didn't care what people thought of me anymore. It was a game-changer for me. Now, I love my colour, enjoy my curls and love being different.

I am proud to be guaranteed Irish and proud of my Jamaican heritage too. When I look in the mirror, I see a brown person: half Black, half white. To me, this means something special and beautiful. I am mixed-race, and I represent what happens when a man and a woman see beyond stereotypes, reach across the racial divide and fall madly in love. I'm proud to say my nanny did that, and so did my ma.

Right now, as I come to the end of our story, that memory of us surrounding Nanny and celebrating her life and times is foremost in my mind. As an actor and filmmaker, I can't think of a better closing scene than Nanny's birthday party. The candles are still flickering on her cake, and we're all singing and laughing and revelling in coming together again after a long time apart.

And as the camera pans around all the people I love most in the world, I can see every hue of hair and skin colour. We're brown and white and black and blonde and grey and brunette and everything in between, but above all, we're family: a strong, united, multiracial, modern, extended, mad Irish family.

I mean, how bloody wonderful is that?

Acknowledgements

KATHLEEN JORDAN

In loving memory of my dear father, Joseph Jordan and my beautiful brother Joseph.

Thanks to my daughter, my two sons, my foster-son, my eight grandchildren and great-grandchild – you are all amazing and much-cherished people in my life. Thank you to my neighbours in Whitestown. I feel so lucky to be surrounded by such wonderful and caring people, and I can't thank you enough for all that you do for me.

DOMINIQUE JORDAN

I want to take this opportunity to thank my mum for bringing up three children on her own in such hard times and for overcoming all the many obstacles in her way. Thank you, Mum, for the unconditional love and support you always show my girls and me.

Thank you to my two brothers and my foster brother, who have shared so much of my journey.

Thanks to my beautiful nieces and nephews, Donna, Monique, Josh, Jayden, Lexee and Cole, and my great-nephew David. I am proud of you all.

Thanks to the Days – Stella, Noel and their family, including my only sister, Laura, and my beautiful goddaughter, Lucy, and her brother, Lee.

To all the strong women of the inner city who made me who I am today, I thank you.

I want to add special thanks to my cousins Sean, his wife Tina and Susie for always keeping me a part of your family.

Lastly, a huge thank you to my girls Jade and Pariss, both strong, loving, beautiful, caring and independent young women. I'm so proud of both of you. What you continue to achieve never fails to amaze me, and as I always say, the world is your oyster.

JADE JORDAN

Where do I start? What a crazy experience this entire process has been – I'm still trying to digest it all! I've experienced a rollercoaster of emotions while writing this book and working to achieve this dream of telling our family story.

Firstly, thanks, Ma, for allowing and trusting me to go on this journey with you. I understand the bravery that this requires, and I'm so proud of you. I honestly feel like a lucky woman to have you as a role model in life, and I'm in absolute awe of what you have achieved and have done for Pariss and me. Your love, support and your guidance mean the world to me.

Thanks also to Nanny for allowing me to delve into your past and embark on this journey together. You are a true hero, and I appreciate all your love and constant support.

Thank you to my beautiful sister, Pariss, for always being by my side, being my best friend and being the very honest person you are. You make me proud every day.

Thank you to the amazing Heffernan family for being my ever-supportive, extended family. All the love in the world goes to my wonderful friends and family for listening to me throughout this process. I am blessed with the absolute best, and I'm so unbelievably grateful to you all.

While writing this book, the one person who was there in spirit with us, giving us all the encouraging smiles we needed, was my great-uncle Joseph. We love and miss you dearly, Joseph, and thank you for being you.

A massive thank you to Hachette Ireland for this amazing opportunity. Thank you Ciara Doorley for approaching me and believing in my family's story. Lastly, Kathryn Rogers, I thank you for working with us on this and bringing our story to life with such talent and passion. Wow, I am grateful!